Fodor's 92
Pocket
Washington,
D.C.

D0423495

Reprinted from *Fodor's Washington, D.C.* '92

Fodor's Travel Publications, Inc.
New York and London

ISBN 0-679-02219-8

First Edition

Fodor's Pocket Washington, D.C.

Editor: Carolyn Price
Editorial Contributors: Bob Blake, Thomas Head, John F. Kelly
Art Director: Fabrizio LaRocca
Cartographer: David Lindroth
Illustrator: Karl Tanner
Cover Photograph: Robert Llewellyn

Design: Vignelli Associates

Special Sales

Fodor's Travel Publications are available at special discounts for bulk purchases (100 copies or more) for sales promotions or premiums. Special editions, including personalized covers, excerpts of existing guides, and corporate imprints, can be created in large quantities for special needs. For more information, write to Special Marketing, Fodor's Travel Publications, 201 E. 50th Street, New York, NY 10022, or call 1–800–800–3246.

MANUFACTURED IN THE UNITED STATES OF AMERICA

10 9 8 7 6 5 4 3 2

Contents

Foreword

While every care has been taken to ensure the accuracy of the information in this guide, the passage of time will always bring change, and consequently the publisher cannot accept responsibility for errors that may occur.

All prices and opening times quoted here are based on information supplied to us at press time. Hours and admission fees may change, however, and the prudent traveler will avoid inconvenience by calling ahead.

Fodor's wants to hear about your travel experiences, both pleasant and unpleasant. When a hotel or restaurant fails to live up to its billing, let us know and we will investigate the complaint and revise our entries where the facts warrant it.

Send your letters to the editors of Fodor's Travel Publications, 201 E. 50th Street, New York, NY 10022.

Washington, D.C. Area

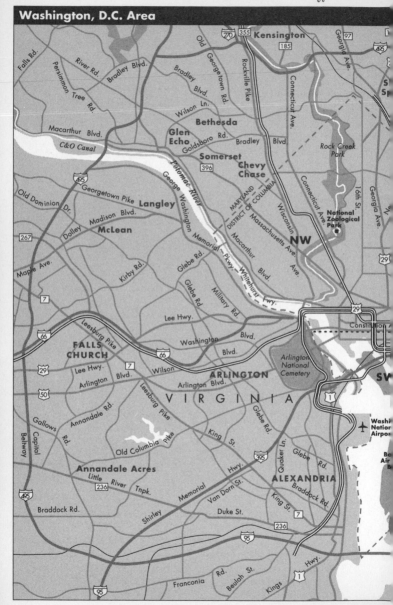

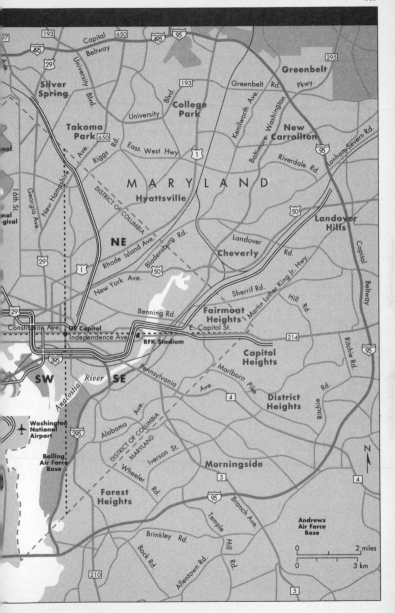

Washington, D.C.

S St.

Decatur Pl.

R St.

Sheridan Circle

Massachusetts Ave.

Q St.

Florida Ave.

New Hampshire Ave.

S St.

R St.

Corcoran St.

Q St.

16th St.

15th St.

14th St.

DUPONT CIRCLE Ⓜ

Church St.

Church St.

Logan Circle

27th St.

Q St.

Rock Creek

O St.

22nd St.

21st St.

20th St.

19th St.

18th St.

Dupont Circle

P St.

17th St.

O St.

N St.

Rhode Island Ave.

13th St.

12th St.

O

29

M St.

New Hampshire Ave.

M St.

M St.

Connecticut Ave.

N St.

Scott Circle

Thomas Circle

Massachusett

26th St.

25th St.

L St.

L St.

15th St.

L St.

Washington Circle

29

FARRAGUT NORTH Ⓜ

FOGGY BOTTOM

K St.

K St.

Ⓜ **FARRAGUT WEST**

16th St.

McPHERSON SQUARE Ⓜ

O

I-66

Ⓜ

Pennsylvania Ave.

H St.

New York Ave.

24th St.

23rd St.

22nd St.

G St.

METRO CENTER Ⓜ

15th St.

14th St.

Virginia Ave.

F St.

The White House

E St.

D St.

17th St.

C St.

FEDERAL TRIANGLE Ⓜ

50 1

50

Constitution Ave.

National Museum of American History

50 1

Vietnam Veterans Memorial

Madison Dr.

N of S

Washington Monument

SMITHSONIAN Ⓜ

Lincoln Memorial

Reflecting Pool

Arlington Memorial Br.

Independence Ave.

Kutz Br.

West

W. Basin Dr.

Ohio Dr.

Potomac Park

Tidal Basin

Potomac River

Outlet Br.

bia d

N

Jefferson Memorial

1

Francis Case Memorial Br

395

NW

SW

S St.

R St.

Rhode Island Ave.

Florida Ave.

S St. **NW** ◆ **NE**

Lincoln Rd.

Q St.

R St.

Logan
Circle

O St.

Q St.

New Jersey Ave.

3rd St.

1st St.

P St.

O St.

9th St.

N St.

13th St.
12th St.
11th St.
10th St.
8th St.
7th St.
6th St.
5th St.
4th St.

New York Ave.

1st St.

M St.

N St.

Massachusetts Ave.

L St.

M St.

North Capitol St.

M St.

Mt. Vernon
Square

I St.

New Jersey

Massachusetts Ave.

2nd St.

SON

ork Ave.

H St.

Ave.

**UNION
STATION**

○ Columbus
Fountain

**METRO
CENTER**

F St.

G St.

**GALLERY
PLACE**

E St.

**JUDICIARY
SQUARE**

395

ERAL
NGLE

50 1

D St.

ARCHIVES
Pennsylvania Ave.

Louisiana Ave.

NE
▲
▼
SE

adison Dr.

**National Museum
of Natural History**
Smithsonian
Institute

**National Gallery
of Art**

● **US
Capitol**

E. Capitol St.

HSONIAN

THE MALL

Jefferson Dr.

**National
Air and Space
Museum**

Independence Ave.

Maryland Ave.

Canal St.

C St.

**L'ENFANT
PLAZA**

D St.

**FEDERAL
CENTER**

w Jersey Ave.

**CAPITOL
SOUTH**
E St.

Virginia Ave.

Southwest Fwy.

G St.

395

395

SW ◆ **SE**

0   500 yards

0   500 meters

Francis Case
Memorial Br.

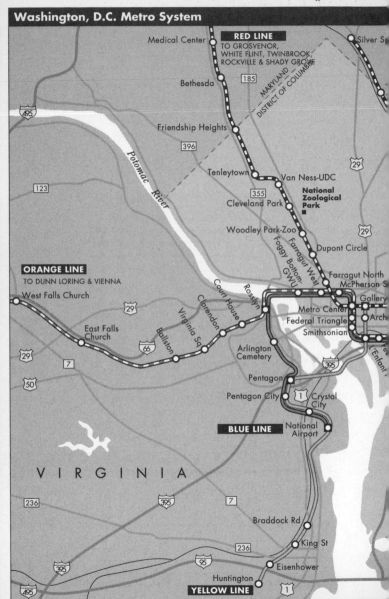

Washington, D.C. Metro System

RED LINE
TO GROSVENOR,
WHITE FLINT, TWINBROOK,
ROCKVILLE & SHADY GROVE

Medical Center

Silver S

Bethesda

185

MARYLAND
DISTRICT OF COLUMBIA

495

Friendship Heights

396

29

Potomac River

123

Tenleytown

Van Ness-UDC

355

**National
Zoological
Park** ■

Cleveland Park

Woodley Park-Zoo

29

Dupont Circle

Foggy Bottom-GWU

Farragut West

ORANGE LINE
TO DUNN LORING & VIENNA

West Falls Church

29

Rosslyn

Court House

Farragut North
McPherson S

Clarendon

Gallery

East Falls
Church

66

Ballston

Virginia Sq

Metro Center

Federal Triangle

Arch

7

Arlington
Cemetery

Smithsonian

50

395

VIRGINIA

Pentagon

l'Enfant F

Pentagon City

1

Crystal
City

236

395

7

BLUE LINE

National
Airport

236

Braddock Rd

95

King St

Eisenhower

495

Huntington

YELLOW LINE

1

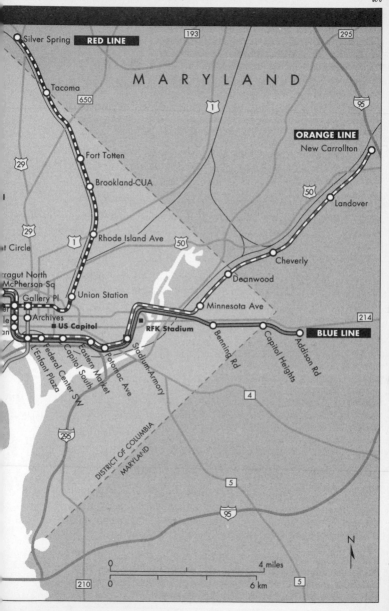

Silver Spring — **RED LINE**

M A R Y L A N D

193

295

Tacoma

650

Fort Totten

Brookland-CUA

ORANGE LINE
New Carrollton

95

50

Landover

Rhode Island Ave

50

Cheverly

29

1

29

t Circle

Deanwood

ragut North
McPherson Sq

Union Station

Minnesota Ave

214

Gallery Pl

Archives

US Capitol

RFK Stadium

BLUE LINE

le
an

Capitol Heights

Addison Rd

Eastern Market

Potomac Ave

Benning Rd

Federal Center SW

Capitol South

Stadium-Armory

L'Enfant Plaza

295

4

DISTRICT OF COLUMBIA
MARYLAND

5

95

N

0   4 miles

0   6 km

210

5

I-29

US 1

Introduction

by Deborah Papier

Deborah Papier is a native Washingtonian who has worked as an editor and writer for numerous local newspapers and magazines.

To a surprising degree, Washington is a city much like any other. True, it does not have a baseball team, that sine qua non of an urban identity. But in most other respects, life in the nation's capital is not that different from life elsewhere in the nation. People are born here, grow up, get jobs—by no means invariably with the federal government— and have children who repeat the cycle. Very often, they live out their lives without ever testifying before Congress, being indicted for influence peddling, or attending a state dinner at the White House.

Which is not to say that the federal government does not cast a long shadow over the city. Among Washington's 630,000 inhabitants are an awful lot of lawyers, journalists, and people who include the word "policy" in their job titles. It's just that DC—to use the vernacular—is much more of a hometown than most tourists realize.

Just a few blocks away from the monuments and museums on the Mall are residential and business districts whose scale is very human. The houses are a crazy quilt of architectural styles, kept in linear formation by rows of lush trees. On the commercial streets, bookstores and ethnic groceries abound.

It is often said that Washington does not have any, "real" neighborhoods, the way nearby Baltimore does. While it's true that Washingtonians are not given to huddling together on their front stoops, each area of the city does have a clearly defined personality.

Sometimes, this personality is a split one. Take Georgetown, for example. One of the city's most in-bred, exclusive communities, its residents successfully fought to keep out the subway. Georgetown is a magnet for the young and the restless from miles around. On any day of the week the streets are full of teenagers with dripping ice cream cones. Friday and Saturday nights it's almost impossible to make your way through the crowds of tourists and natives. Halloween in Georgetown is as close as Washington gets to Mardi Gras, though things aren't quite as weird and wild as they were a few years ago.

Another distinctive neighborhood is Dupont Circle. Insofar as there is a bohemian Washington, it can be found here. This is where the artists and activists used to live, before the rents got too high, and where the hippies hung out, back at the dawning of the New Age. Now Dupont Circle is home to the most visible segment of Washington's gay community.

Adjacent to Dupont Circle is Adams-Morgan, long the city's most intensely ethnic neighborhood. In recent years Adams-Morgan has begun to lose some of its Hispanic flavor, as New American restaurants have begun to crowd out the Latin places. But you're still likely to hear more Spanish than English on the streets here.

As different as Georgetown, Dupont Circle, and Adams-Morgan are, they have one thing in common. They are all on the same side of the line that divides white from black Washington. With the exception of Capitol Hill, whites live west of 16th Street, while blacks—who make up the majority of the population—live to the east of it.

That's a long-standing demographic pattern, unchanged despite the supposed advent of integration. Whites and blacks now work together in the downtown offices, but they go off in different directions when they head home, and rarely encounter one another when they go out for the evening. At the Kennedy Center, for example, there are few black faces to be found.

Meanwhile, there is no comparable center for black culture. The riots of 1968 wiped out most of the black clubs and businesses, and while the area around 14th and U streets where they once flourished is finally being rebuilt, its vitality is unlikely to be re-created.

Further down on 14th Street, another aspect of Washington life is breathing its last: The 14th Street red-light district is almost gone. The city was determined to clean up the strip, and to everyone's surprise it succeeded.

Nor is much left of the tacky commercial district around 9th and F streets. This was Washington's original downtown, which deteriorated when the city's center shifted to the west, to the "new" downtown of Connecticut Avenue and K Street. But the "old" downtown is being rejuvenated. The department stores that once drew crowds with their window displays have been renovated; there are new hotels and office buildings; and as the construction dust clears, the area is looking pretty good.

There is still work to be done, however. Seventh Street, for example, is a particular eyesore. It was hoped that this street would develop into a downtown arts district. But the gallery row that was envisioned for it has not materialized as planned, leaving the future of the street in doubt.

But the success or failure of an urban renewal project is probably not a matter of the utmost concern to the visitor. What many people who come here are worried about is crime. Crime is certainly a major problem here, as it is in other big cities, but Washington is not nearly as dangerous as its well-publicized homicide rate might lead you to believe. Most visitors have relatively little to fear. The drug-related shootings that have made Washington the murder capital generally take place in remote sections of the city. Unless you go seeking out the drug markets, there isn't much chance you'll get caught in the cross fire of rival drug gangs. Crimes against property are more widespread, but still far from ubiquitous. Unlike New York, Washington is not full of expert pickpockets; nor is it plagued by gold-chain snatchers.

The city's Metro is generally safe, even at night. However, if you're going to have to walk from your stop in a neighborhood that isn't well-lit and trafficked, you probably should invest in a taxi. Of course, even exercising normal prudence, it is still possible that you will have an encounter with someone who believes that what's yours ought to be his. If that happens, don't argue.

Your attachment to the contents of your wallet is certain to be tested in another way, however. Panhandlers are now a fixture of the cityscape, and there is no avoiding their importunities. How you respond to them is a matter only your conscience can advise you on. Some Washingtonians start the day with a pocketful of quarters, which they dispense to anyone who approaches them—until the money runs out. Other people sometimes give, sometimes don't, presumably according to some moral yardstick invisible to anyone else. Still others, overwhelmed or outraged by the incessant requests for a handout, feign deafness.

Whether or not you choose to dig into your pocket, you needn't feel threatened by the beggars. While they can be quite unsavory-looking, they are almost never aggressive or abusive. They ask for money; they don't demand it. And they accept a refusal, particularly one prefaced with an "I'm sorry," with considerable grace.

But they are changing the face of the city. Wealth and poverty have always coexisted here, but until recently poverty kept its distance. It's now omnipresent, wearing a very human face.

1 Essential Information

Before You Go

Visitor Information

For free brochures, an up-to-date calendar of events, and other general information about the District of Columbia, contact the **Washington Convention and Visitors Association** (1212 New York Ave. NW, Washington, D.C. 20005, tel. 202/789–7000).

If you're planning to visit sites in the surrounding areas of Maryland, contact the **Maryland Department of Economic and Community Development** (Office of Tourist Development, 45 Calvert St., Annapolis, MD 21401, tel. 301/269–3517). For tourist information on Virginia, contact the **Virginia Division of Tourism** (202 N. 9th St., Suite 500, Richmond, VA 23219, tel. 804/786–4484).

When to Go

Washington has two delightful seasons: spring and autumn, each with its own best features. In spring the city's ornamental fruit trees are budding, and its many gardens are in bloom. The Cherry Blossom Festival is held every April—whether or not the pink flowers choose to grace the city with their presence. The Smithsonian Kite Flying Contest behind the Washington Monument and the White House Easter Egg Roll are other popular spring activities. By autumn most of the summer crowds have left and visitors can enjoy the museums, galleries, and timeless monuments in peace.

Summers can be uncomfortably hot and humid (local legend has it that Washington was considered a "tropical hardship post" by some European diplomats), but that doesn't stop thousands of people from converging on the Mall for the annual Smithsonian Festival of American Folklife. Winter witnesses the lighting of the National Christmas Tree and countless historic-house tours, but the winter months are often bitter, with a handful of modest snowstorms that somehow bring this "southern" city to a standstill.

Visitors interested in government will want to visit Washington when Congress is in session. When lawmakers break for recess (for Christmas, Easter, July 4, and other holiday periods), the city seems a little less vibrant.

What follows are the average daily maximum and minimum temperatures for Washington.

Climate								
Jan.	47F	8C	May	76F	24C	Sept.	79F	26C
	34	−1		58	14		61	16
Feb.	47F	8C	June	85F	29C	Oct.	70F	21C
	31	−1		65	18		52	11
Mar.	56F	13C	July	88F	31C	Nov.	56F	13C
	38	3		70	21		41	5
Apr.	67F	19C	Aug.	86F	30C	Dec.	47F	8C
	47	8		68	20		32	0

Festivals and Seasonal Events

Feb.: Black History Month is celebrated at sites around the city; **Late Mar.–Early Apr.: The National Cherry Blossom Festival** sees parades, a marathon, and a beauty contest in celebration of the Japanese cherry trees that ring the Tidal Basin; **Mid-June–Aug.: The Armed Forces Concert Series** offers military band performances nightly on the Capitol and Washington Monument grounds; **Late June: The Festival of American Folklife** on the Mall features the music, food, and arts and crafts of various cutlures; **the Fourth of July** finds thousands of celebrants spread out on the Mall, listening to a band concert then watching fireworks after the sun sets; **Mid-Dec.: The National Christmas Tree Lighting and Pageant** is the start of the holiday season, as the president lights the national tree and the Ellipse behind the White House becomes the site of nightly choral performances.

What to Pack

What you pack depends largely on where you're headed. Washington is basically informal, although many restaurants require a jacket and tie. Theaters and nightclubs in the area range from the slightly dressy (John F. Kennedy Center) to extremely casual (Wolf Trap Farm Park). For sightseeing and casual dining, jeans and sneakers are acceptable just about anywhere. Summer is usually very hot and humid, so you'll want to have shorts and light shirts. Even in August, though, you might still want to have a shawl or light jacket for air-conditioned restaurants. Good walking shoes are a must since most of the city's interesting neighborhoods and sites are best explored on foot. The only really cold months, for which you'll need a heavy coat and snow boots, are January and February.

Carry-on Luggage Passengers on U.S. airlines are limited to two carry-on bags. For a bag you wish to store under the seat, the maximum dimensions are 9″ × 14″ × 22″. For bags that can be hung in a closet or on a luggage rack, the maximum dimensions are 4″ × 23″ × 45″. For bags you wish to store in an overhead bin, the maximum dimensions are 10″ × 14″ × 36″. Any item that exceeds the specified dimensions may be rejected as a carry-on and taken as checked baggage. Keep in mind that an airline can adapt the rules to circumstances, so on an especially crowded flight don't be surprised if you are only allowed one carry-on bag.

In addition to the two carry-ons, you may bring aboard a handbag (pocketbook or purse); an overcoat or wrap; an umbrella; a camera; a reasonable amount of reading material; an infant bag; crutches, cane, braces, or other prosthetic device; and an infant/child safety seat if a ticket has been purchased for the child or if there is space in the cabin.

Checked Luggage Luggage allowances vary slightly from airline to airline. Many carriers allow three checked pieces; some allow only two. Again, it is best to check before you go. In all cases, each piece of checked luggage may not weigh more than 70 pounds or be larger than 62 inches (length + width + height).

Arriving and Departing

By Plane

Airports Most national and international airlines as well as many regional and commuter carriers serve one or more of Washington's three airports. **Na-**

tional Airport, in Virginia, 4 miles south of downtown Washington, is popular with politicians and their staffs. It is often cramped and crowded, but it's convenient to downtown (20 minutes by subway to the Metro Center stop). Many transcontinental and international flights arrive at **Dulles International Airport,** a modern facility 26 miles west of Washington. **Baltimore-Washington International (BWI) Airport** is in Maryland, about 25 miles northeast of Washington. All three airports are served by a variety of bus and limousine companies that make scheduled trips between airports and to downtown Washington.

Airlines When buying your ticket, be sure to distinguish among nonstop flights (no changes, no stops), direct flights (no changes but one or more stops), and connecting flights (two or more planes, two or more stops).

National Airport is served by **America West** (tel. 800/247–5692), **American** (tel. 800/433–7300), **Continental** (tel. 800/525–0280), **Delta** (tel. 800/221–1212), **Midway** (tel. 800/621–5700), **Midwest** (tel. 800/452–2022), **Northwest** (tel. 800/225–2525), **Trump Shuttle** (tel. 800/AIR–TRUM), **TWA** (tel. 800/221–2000), **United** (tel. 800/241–6522), and **USAir** (tel. 800/428–4322).

Major air carriers serving Dulles include **Aeroflot** (tel. 202/429–4922), **Air France** (tel. 800/237–2747), **All Nippon** (tel. 800/2FLY–ANA), **American** (tel. 800/433–7300), **Bahamasair** (tel. 800/222–4262), **British Airways** (tel. 800/247–9297), **Business Express** (tel. 800/345–3400), **Continental** (tel. 800/525–0280), **Delta** (tel. 800/221–1212), **Lufthansa** (tel. 800/645–3880), **Mohawk** (tel. 800/252–2144), **Northwest** (tel. 800/225–2525), **Saudi Arabian** (tel. 800/4SAUDIA), **TWA** (tel. 800/221–2000), **United** (tel. 800/241–6522), **USAir** (tel. 800/428–4322), and **Wings Airways** (tel. 800/648–WINGS).

Airlines that serve BWI include **Air Jamaica** (tel. 800/523–5585), **America West** (tel. 800/247–5692), **American** (tel. 800/433–7300), **Continental** (tel. 800/525–0280), **Cumberland** (tel. 800/624–0070), **Delta** (tel. 800/221–1212), **Enterprise** (tel. 800/327–8376), **Icelandair** (tel. 800/223–5500), **KLM Royal Dutch** (tel. 800/777–5553),

Mexicana (tel. 800/531–7921), **Northwest** (tel. 800/225–2525), **PanAm Express** (tel. 800/221–1111), **TWA** (tel. 800/221–2000), **United** (tel. 800/241–6522) and **USAir** (tel. 800/428–4322).

Between the Airports and Downtown
By Metro If you are coming into Washington National Airport, don't have too much to carry, and are staying at a hotel near a subway stop, it makes sense to take the Metro downtown. You can walk to the station or catch the free airport shuttle that stops at each terminal and brings you to the National Airport station on the Blue and Yellow lines. The Metro ride downtown takes about 20 minutes and costs between $1 and $1.25, depending on the time of day.

By Bus National and Dulles airports are served continuously by the buses of **Washington Flyer** (tel. 703/685–1400). The ride from National to downtown takes 20 minutes and costs $7 ($12 round-trip). From Dulles it's $14 for the hour-long ride ($22 round-trip). An inter-airport express travels between Dulles and National. The 45-minute trip costs $14 ($26 round-trip). Washington Flyer also provides service to various locations in the Maryland and Virginia suburbs.

The Airport Connection (tel. 301/441–2345) serves BWI airport with buses that leave roughly every hour for downtown Washington. The 65-minute ride costs $13 ($23 round-trip).

Some hotels provide van service to and from the airports; check with your hotel when making reservations or when you arrive.

By Train Free shuttle buses take passengers to and from the train station at BWI airport. **Amtrak** and **MARC (Maryland Rail Commuter Service)** trains run between BWI and Washington's Union Station from around 6 AM to 11 PM. The cost for the 40-minute ride is $11 on an Amtrak train, $4.25 on a MARC train (weekdays only). (For Amtrak schedule information, call 800/USA–RAIL; for MARC schedule information, call 800/325–RAIL.)

By Taxi If you're traveling alone, expect to pay about $8 to get from National Airport to downtown; from Dulles, $35; from BWI, $36. Unscrupulous cabbies prey on out-of-towners so if the fare strikes you as astronomical get the driver's name and cab number and threaten to call the D.C. Taxicab Commission (tel. 202/767–8380).

By Limousine Call at least a day ahead and **Diplomat Limousine** (tel. 703/461–6800) will have a limousine waiting for you at the airport. The ride downtown from National costs $33. It costs $60 from Dulles and $117 from BWI. Sedans are about a third cheaper.

By Car

If you are arriving by car note that I–95 skirts Washington as part of the Beltway, the six- to eight-lane highway that encircles the city. The eastern half of the Beltway is I–95, the western half is I–495. If coming from the south, take I–95 to I–395 and cross the 14th Street bridge to 14th Street in the District. From the north, stay on I–95 south before heading west on Route 50, the John Hanson Highway, which turns into New York Avenue.

Car Rentals

Ample public transportation and shuttle service from the airports to downtown make it relatively easy to get by in Washington without renting a car. Traffic is bad, and traffic rules can be confusing even to natives. If a rental car figures in your plans, however, there are plenty of companies to choose from. Most of the major car rental companies—including **Avis** (tel. 800/331–1212), **Budget** (tel. 800/527–0700), **Dollar** (tel. 800/800–4000), **Hertz** (tel. 800/654–3131), and **National** (tel. 800/328–4567)—have offices at the three airports and in the downtown hotel/business district.

By Train

More than 50 trains a day arrive at Washington's restored **Union Station** on Capitol Hill (50 Massachusetts Ave. NE, tel. 202/484–7540 or 800/USA–RAIL). Washington is the last stop on Amtrak's Northeast Corridor line and is a major stop on most routes from the south and west. Metroliner trains travel between New York and Washington five times every weekday.

By Bus

Washington is a major terminal for **Greyhound/
Trailways Bus Lines** (1005 1st St. NE, tel. 301/
565–2662). The company also has stations in
nearby Silver Spring and Laurel, Maryland,
and in Springfield, Virginia. Check with your
local Greyhound/Trailways ticket office for
prices and schedules.

Staying in Washington

Important Addresses and Numbers

Because of the booming growth in Washington
and its surrounding Maryland and Virginia suburbs, you must now use the area code (without
first dialing 1) when calling locally between any
of the three jurisdictions: 202 for Washington,
301 for Maryland, and 703 for Virginia.

Tourist Information The **Washington, D.C. Convention and Visitors
Association** operates a tourist information cen-
ter at 1455 Pennsylvania Avenue, NW (tel. 202/
789–7000; tel. 202/737–8866 for recorded an-
nouncement of upcoming events). The **International Visitor Information Service** (733 15th St.
NW, Suite 300, tel. 202/783–6540) answers for-
eigners' questions about Washington and has
maps and brochures on area attractions in eight
languages. Rangers from the National Park
Service staff information-kiosks on the Mall,
near the White House, next to the Vietnam Veterans Memorial, and at several other locations
throughout the city. **Dial-A-Park** (tel. 202/619–
PARK) is a recording of events at Park Service
attractions in and around Washington. If you're
planning on doing any sightseeing in Virginia,
stop by the **Virginia Travel Center** (1629 K St.
NW, tel. 202/659–5523). If Maryland figures in
your travel plans, contact the state's **Office of
Tourist Development** (tel. 301/333–6611; for Baltimore information specifically, tel. 800/282–
6632).

Emergencies Dial 911 for assistance. The hospital closest to
downtown is **George Washington University Hos-
pital** (901 23rd St. NW, tel. 202/994–3211).

Doctors and Dentists **Prologue** (tel. 202/DOCTORS) is a referral service that locates doctors, dentists, and urgent-care clinics in the greater Washington area. The **DC Dental Society** (tel. 202/547–7615) operates a referral line weekdays 8 to 4.

Late-night Pharmacies **Peoples Drug** operates two 24-hour pharmacies in the District. One is at 14th Street and Thomas Circle NW (tel. 202/628–0720), the other at 7 Dupont Circle NW (tel. 202/785–1466).

Getting Around Washington

By Subway The **Washington Metropolitan Area Transit Authority** (WMATA) provides bus and subway service in the District and in the Maryland and Virginia suburbs. The **Metro,** opened in 1976, is one of the country's cleanest and safest subway systems. Trains run from 5:30 AM to midnight, Monday through Friday; 8 AM to midnight on Saturdays; 10 AM to midnight on Sundays. During the weekday rush hours (5:30–9:30 AM and 3–7 PM) trains come along every six minutes. At other times and on weekends and holidays trains run about every 12 to 15 minutes. The base fare is $1; the actual price you pay depends on the time of day and the distance traveled. Children under five ride free when accompanied by a paying passenger, but there is a maximum of two children per paying adult.

The computerized **Farecard machines** in Metro stations can seem complicated. You'll need a pocketful of coins or crisp one- or five-dollar bills to feed into the machines; machines in some stations also accept $10 and $20 bills. If the machine spits your bill back out at you, try folding and unfolding it before asking a native for help. The paper Farecard you purchase should be inserted into the turnstile to enter the platform. Make sure you hang onto the card—you'll need it to exit at your destination.

An $8 **Metro Family/Tourist Pass** entitles a family of four to one day of unlimited subway and bus travel any Saturday, Sunday, or holiday (except July 4). Passes are available at Metro Sales Outlets (including the Metro Center station) and at many hotels.

For general travel information, tel. 202/637–7000 or TTD 202/638–3780 seven days a week 6 AM to 11:30 PM; for consumer assistance, tel. 202/637–1328; for transit police, tel. 202/962–2121. A helpful brochure—"All About the Metro System"—is available by calling the travel information number or writing to: Office of Marketing, WMATA, 600 5th St. NW, Washington, D.C. 20001.

By Bus WMATA's red, white, and blue **Metrobuses** crisscross the city and nearby suburbs, with some routes running 24 hours a day. All bus rides within the District are $1.

Free transfers, good for two hours, are available on buses and in Metro stations. Bus-to-bus transfers are accepted at designated Metrobus transfer points. Rail-to-bus transfers must be picked up before boarding the train. There may be a transfer charge when boarding the bus. There are no bus-to-rail transfers.

By Car A car can be a drawback in Washington. Traffic is horrendous, especially at rush hours, and driving is often confusing, with many lanes and some entire streets changing direction suddenly at certain times of day. Parking is also an adventure; the police are quick to tow away or immobilize with a "boot" any vehicle parked illegally. Since the city's most popular sights are within a short walk of a Metro station anyway, it's best to leave your car at the hotel. Touring by car is a good idea only if you're considering visiting sites in suburban Maryland or Virginia.

By Taxi Taxis in the District are not metered; they operate instead on a curious zone system. Even longtime Washingtonians will ask the cabdriver ahead of time how much the fare will be. The basic single rate for traveling within one zone is $3. There is an extra $1.25 charge for each additional passenger and a $1 surcharge during the 4 to 6:30 PM rush hour. Bulky suitcases larger than three cubic feet are charged at a higher rate and a $1.50 surcharge is tacked on when you phone for a cab. Two major companies serving the District are **Capitol Cab** (tel. 202/546–2400) and **Diamond Cab** (tel. 202/387–6200). Maryland and Virginia taxis are metered but cannot take passengers between points in Washington.

Guided Tours

Orientation Tours Taking a narrated bus tour is a good way to get your bearings and make some decisions about what to see first. Both of the tour companies listed here allow you to get off and on as often as you like with no additional charge. If you want to conserve your energy for walking inside Washington's museums, art galleries, and other touring sights, rather than walking *between* them, a bus tour is the way to go.

Tourmobile (tel. 202/554–7950 or 202/554–5100). Authorized by the National Park Service, Tourmobile buses ply a route that stops at 18 historic sites between the Capitol and Arlington Cemetery; the route includes the White House and the museums on the Mall. Tickets are $8 for adults, $4 for children 3–11.

Old Town Trolley Tours (tel. 202/269–3020). Orange-and-green motorized trolleys take in the main downtown sights and also foray into Georgetown and the upper northwest, stopping at out-of-the-way attractions like the Washington Cathedral. Tickets are $14 for adults, $5 for children 5 to 12, and free for the under 5 set.

Bus Tours **Gray Line Tours** (tel. 301/386–8300). A four-hour motorcoach tour of Washington, Embassy Row, and Arlington National Cemetery leaves Union Station at 8:30 AM and 2:30 PM (at 2 PM November–March); tours of Mount Vernon and Alexandria depart at 9 AM (adults $20, children 2 to 12, $10). An all-day trip combining both tours leaves at 8:30 AM (adults $36, children $18).

River Tours *Spirit of Washington* (Pier 4, 6th and Water Sts. SW, tel. 202/554–8000 or 202/554–1542). Moored at the heart of Washington's waterfront, this boat gives visitors a waterborne view of some of the area's attractions, including Old Town Alexandria, Washington National Airport, and Hains Point. Lunch cruises board Tuesday through Saturday at 11:30 AM; a Sunday brunch cruise sails at 1. Evening cruises board at 6:30 PM and include dinner and a floor show. Adult "moonlight party cruises" leave Friday and Saturday at 11 PM. Prices range from $17 per person for the moonlight cruise to $38.95 for dinner on a Friday or Saturday night.

A sister ship, the *Spirit of Mt. Vernon,* sails to George Washington's plantation home from mid-March to early October, Tuesday through Sunday. The four-hour trip embarks at 9 AM and 2 PM.

2 Exploring Washington

Orientation

by John F. Kelly

John F. Kelly is an editor for the Washington Post's *Weekend section.*

The city's streets are arranged, said Pierre L'Enfant, the man who designed them in 1791, "like a chessboard overlaid with a wagon wheel." Streets run north and south and east and west in a grid pattern; avenues—most named after states—run diagonally, connecting the various traffic circles scattered throughout the city. The District is divided into four sections: northwest, northeast, southwest, and southeast; the Capitol Building serves as the center of the north/south and east/west axes. North Capitol and South Capitol streets divide the city into east and west; the Mall and East Capitol Street divide the city into north and south. Streets that run north to south are numbered; those that extend east to west are lettered from A to I and K to W, the letter J having been skipped. (Note that I Street is often written as "Eye Street.") After W, two-syllable alphabetical names are used for east/west streets (Adams, Belmont, Clifton, etc.), then three-syllable names (Albemarle, Brandywine, Chesapeake). After the three-syllable names to the north have been exhausted, the streets are named for trees (Aspen, Butternut, Cedar).

Make sure you have a destination's complete address, including the quadrant designation. There are four 4th and D Street intersections in Washington: one each in NW, NE, SW, and SE. Addresses in Washington are coded to the intersections they're closest to. For example, 1785 Massachusetts Ave. NW is between 17th and 18th Streets; 600 5th St. NW is at the corner of 5th and F, the sixth letter of the alphabet.

Tour 1: The Mall

Numbers in the margin correspond to points of interest on the Tour 1: The Mall map.

The Mall is the heart of nearly every visitor's trip to Washington. With nine diverse museums ringing the expanse of green, it's the closest thing the capital has to a theme park (unless you count the Federal government itself, which has uncharitably been called "Disneyland on the Potomac"). As at a theme park, you may have to stand in an occasional line, but unlike the amusements at Disneyland almost everything you'll see here is free.

The Mall is bounded on the north and south by Constitution and Independence avenues, and on the east and west by 4th and 14th streets. Nearly all of the Smithsonian museums lie within these boundaries. (Nearest Metro stop, Smithsonian or Archives.)

The best place to start an exploration of the museums on the Mall is in front of the first one constructed, the **Smithsonian Institution Building.** British scientist and founder James Smithson had never visited America. Yet his will stipulated that, should his nephew, Henry James Hungerford, die without an heir, Smithson's entire fortune would go to the United States, "to found at Washington, under the name of the Smithsonian Institution, an establishment for the increase and diffusion of knowledge among men."

Smithson died in 1829, Hungerford in 1835, and in 1838 the United States received $515,169 worth of gold sovereigns. After eight years of Congressional debate over the propriety of accepting funds from a private citizen, the Smithsonian Institution was finally established in 1846. The red sandstone, Norman-style headquarters building on Jefferson Drive was completed in 1855 and originally housed all of the Smithsonian's operations, including the science and art collections, research laboratories, and living quarters for the Institution's secretary and his family. Known as "the Castle," the building was designed by James Renwick, the architect of St. Patrick's Cathedral in New York City.

Today the Castle houses Smithsonian administrative offices and is home to the Woodrow Wilson International School for Scholars. To get your bearings or to get help deciding which Mall attractions you want to devote your time to, visit the new **Smithsonian Information Center** in the Castle. An orientation film provides an overview of the various Smithsonian museums and monitors display information on the day's events. The Information Center opens at 9 AM,

Exploring Washington, D.C.

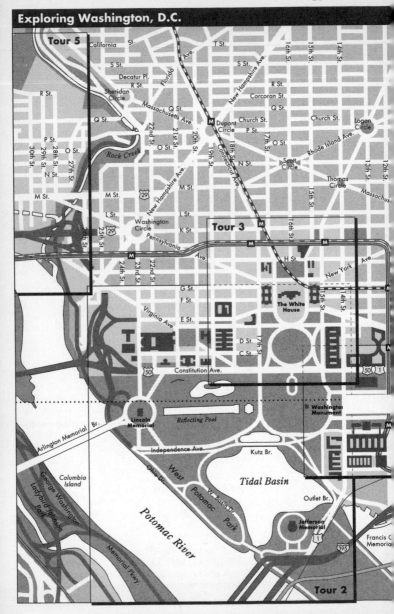

Tour 5

California St.
T St.
S St.
15th St.
14th St.
New Hampshire Ave.
Decatur Pl.
R St.
Sheridan Circle
Florida
R St.
Corcoran St.
R St.
16th St.
Q St.
Massachusetts Ave.
Q St.
Church St.
Q St.
Church St.
Logan Circle
Dupont Circle
P St.
17th St.
Connecticut Ave.
Rhode Island Ave.
P St.
O St.
O St.
20th St.
21st St.
22nd St.
N St.
Scott Circle
13th St.
12th St.
Rock Creek
Thomas Circle
Massachus.
30th St.
29th St.
28th St.
27th St.
P St.
O St.
N St.
M St.
29
M St.
M St.
M St.
15th St.
L St.
L St.
Tour 3
16th St.
New Hampshire Ave.
25th St.
29
Washington Circle
K St.
Pennsylvania
H St.
New York Ave.
Ave.
24th St.
23rd St.
22nd St.
G St.
F St.
The White House
15th St.
14th St.
Virginia Ave.
E St.
17th St.
D St.
C St.
50
Constitution Ave.
Reflecting Pool
Washington Monument
Lincoln Memorial
Arlington Memorial Br.
Independence Ave.
Kutz Br.
Columbia Island
Ohio Dr.
West
Potomac
Park
Tidal Basin
George Washington
Lady Bird Johnson
Park
W. Basin Dr.
Outlet Br.
Memorial Pkwy.
Potomac River
Jefferson Memorial
395
Francis C
Memorial
Tour 2

NW ◀▶ NE

T St.

S St.

Rhode Island Ave.

R St.

Florida Ave.

Q St.

Logan Circle

O St.

N St.

Lincoln Rd.

R St.

Q St.

O St.

New Jersey Ave.

3rd St.

1st St.

P St.

New York Ave.

M St.

3rd St.

13th St. 12th St. 11th St. 10th St. 9th St. 8th St. 7th St. 6th St. 5th St. 4th St.

N St.

M St.

L St.

Massachusetts Ave.

Mt. Vernon Square

New Jersey Ave.

North Capitol St.

1st St.

50

I St.

H St.

Massachusetts   Ave.

2nd St.

Tour 4

G St.

F St.

Union Station

E St.

395

Columbus Fountain

Pennsylvania

Ave.

D St.

Stanton Park

Madison Dr.

National Gallery of Art

US Capitol

NE ◀▶ SE

Smithsonian Institute

THE MALL

Jefferson Dr.

National Air and Space Museum

E. Capitol St.

Independence Ave.

Maryland Ave.

Folger Park

C St.

Canal St.

Tour 1

CAPITOL SOUTH

D St.

E St.

395

New Jersey Ave.

Virginia Ave.

Southwest Fwy.

G St.

395

Francis Case Memorial Br.

I St.

Washington Canal

0   500 yards

SW ◀▶ SE

0   500 meters

N

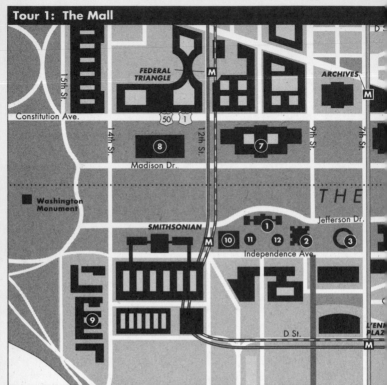

Tour 1: The Mall

Arthur M.
Sackler
Gallery, **11**

Arts and
Industries
Building, **2**

Bureau of
Engraving and
Printing, **9**

Freer Gallery
of Art, **10**

Hirshhorn
Museum and
Sculpture
Garden, **3**

National Air and
Space
Museum, **4**

National Gallery
of Art, east
building, **6**

National Gallery
of Art, west
building, **5**

National
Museum of
African Art, **12**

National
Museum of
American
History, **8**

National
Museum of
Natural
History, **7**

Smithsonian
Institution
Building, **1**

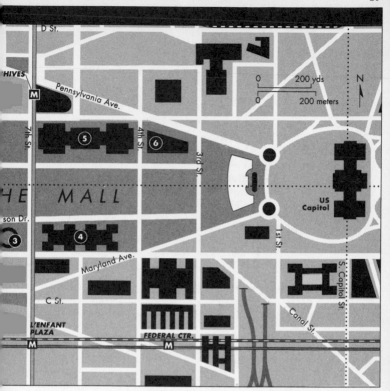

an hour before the other museums open, so you can plan your day on the Mall without wasting valuable sightseeing time. *1000 Jefferson Dr. SW, tel. 202/357–2700. Open daily 9–5:30.*

To the right of the Castle is the pagoda-like entrance to the **S. Dillon Ripley Center,** an underground collection of classrooms and offices named after a past Smithsonian secretary. Works from around the world are periodically shown in the center's International Gallery.

This tour circles the Mall counterclockwise. Start by walking east on Jefferson Drive to the ❷ **Arts and Industries Building,** the second Smithsonian museum to be constructed. In 1876 Philadelphia hosted the United States International Exposition in honor of the nation's Centennial. After the festivities, scores of exhibitors donated their displays to the Federal government. In order to house the objects that had suddenly come its way, the Smithsonian commissioned this redbrick and sandstone building. Designed by Adolph Cluss, the building was originally called the United States National Museum, the name that is still engraved in stone above the doorway. It was finished in 1881, just in time for President James Garfield's inaugural ball.

The Arts and Industries Building exhibits an extensive collection of American Victoriana; many of the objects on display—which include carriages, tools, furnishings, printing presses, even a steam locomotive—are from the original Philadelphia Centennial. In 1991 the Smithsonian opened the Experimental Gallery in the south quadrant of the Arts and Industries Building. The gallery is a laboratory that allows museum curators to experiment not so much with *what* should be displayed but *how* to display it. *900 Jefferson Dr. SW, tel. 202/357–2700. Open daily 10–5:30.*

❸ The **Hirshhorn Museum** is the next building to the east on Jefferson Drive, and you would be hard pressed to find a piece of architecture that contrasts more with the gay Victoriana of the Arts and Industries Building. Dubbed "the Doughnut on the Mall," the reinforced-concrete building designed by Gordon Bunshaft is a fitting home for contemporary—and sometimes controversial—art. Opened in 1974, the museum manages a collection of 4,000 paintings and drawings and 2,000 sculptures. American artists such as Eakins, Pollock, Rothko, and Stella are represented, as are modern European and Latin masters, including Francis Bacon, Fernando Botero, Magritte, Miró, and Victor Vasarely.

The Hirshhorn's impressive sculpture collection is arranged in the open spaces between the museum's concrete piers and across Jefferson Drive in the sunken **Sculpture Garden.** The display in the Sculpture Garden includes the largest public American collection of works by Henry Moore, as well as works by Henri Daumier, Max Ernst, Alberto Giacometti, Pablo Picasso, and Man Ray. Auguste Rodin's *The Burghers of Calais* is a highlight. *Independence Ave. at 7th St. SW, tel. 202/357-2700. Open daily 10-5:30. Extended spring/summer hours determined annually. Sculpture garden open daily 7:30-dusk.*

❹ Cross 7th Street to get to the **National Air and Space Museum.** Opened in 1976, Air and Space is the most visited museum in the world, attracting 12 million people each year. (It's thought to be the single most-visited building on earth.) Twenty-three galleries tell the story of aviation, from man's earliest attempts at flight to his travels beyond our solar system. Suspended from the ceiling like plastic models in a child's room are dozens of aircraft, including the actual *Wright Flyer* that Wilbur Wright piloted over the sands of Kitty Hawk, North Carolina; Charles Lindbergh's *Spirit of St. Louis*; the X-1 rocket plane in which Chuck Yeager broke the sound barrier; and the X-15, the fastest plane ever built.

Don't let long lines deter you from seeing a show in the museum's **Langley Theater.** IMAX films shown on the five-story-high screen—including *The Dream is Alive, To Fly!, On the Wing,* and *The Blue Planet*—usually feature swooping aerial scenes that will convince you you've left the ground. Buy your tickets ($2.75 for adults; $1.75 for children, students, and senior citizens) as soon as you arrive, then look around the museum. Upstairs, the **Albert Einstein Planetarium** projects images of celestial bodies on a domed ceiling. *Jefferson Dr. at Sixth St. SW, tel. 202/357–2700. Open daily 10–5:30. Specially priced double features are often shown in the Langley Theater after the museum has closed. For information, call 202/357–1686.*

Time Out   Two restaurants opened in 1988 in the eastern end of the National Air and Space Museum. **The Wright Place** is a table-service restaurant that takes reservations (tel. 202/371–8777); the **Flight Line** is a self-service cafeteria. They each have a large selection of foods, but at peak times lines can be long.

After touring the Air and Space Museum, walk east on Jefferson Drive toward the Capitol. What has been called the last open space left for a museum on the periphery of the Mall is bounded by 3rd and 4th streets and Independence Avenue and Jefferson Drive SW. The Smithsonian's **National Museum of the American Indian** is scheduled to open here in 1998.

To get to the museums on the north side of the Mall, walk north on 4th or 3rd Street. As you walk, look to the left for a good view of the Mall. Notice how the Castle projects slightly into the green rectangle. When it was built, in 1855, Pierre L'Enfant's plan for Washington had been all but forgotten. In this space west of the "Congress House," the Frenchman had envisioned a "Grand Avenue, 400 feet in breadth, and about a mile in length, bordered with gardens, ending in a slope from the houses on each side." In the middle of the 19th century, horticulturalist Andrew Jackson Downing took a stab at converting the Mall into a large, English-style garden, with carriageways curving through groves of trees and bushes. This was far from the "vast esplanade" L'Enfant had in mind, and by the dawn of the 20th century the Mall had become an eyesore. It was dotted with sheds and bisected by railroad tracks. There was even a railroad station at its eastern end.

In 1900 Senator James McMillan, chairman of the Committee on the District of Columbia,

asked a distinguished group of architects and
artists to study ways of improving Washington's
park system. The McMillan Commission, which
included architects Daniel Burnham and
Charles McKim, landscape architect Frederick
Law Olmsted, Jr., and sculptor Augustus Saint-
Gaudens, didn't confine its recommendations
just to parks; its 1902 report would shape the
way the capital looked for decades. The Mall received much of the group's attention and is its
most stunning accomplishment. L'Enfant's plan
was rediscovered, the sheds, railroad tracks,
and carriageways were removed, and Washington finally had the monumental core it had been
denied for so long.

⑤ Cross Madison Drive to get to the two buildings
of the **National Gallery of Art,** one of the world's
foremost collections of paintings, sculptures,
and graphics. If you want to view the museum's
holdings in (more or less) chronological order,
it's best to start your exploration of this magnif-
icent gallery in the **west building.** Opened in
1941, the domed building was a gift to the nation
from financier Andrew Mellon. Mellon had long
collected great works of art, acquiring them on
his frequent trips to Europe. In 1931, when the
Soviet government was short on cash and selling
off many of its art treasures, Mellon stepped in
and bought $6 million worth of Old Masters,
including *The Alba Madonna* by Raphael and
Botticelli's *Adoration of the Magi.* Mellon prom-
ised his collection to America in 1937, the year of
his death. He also donated the funds for the construction of the huge gallery and resisted sug-
gestions it be named after him.

The west building's **Great Rotunda,** with its 16
marble columns surrounding a fountain topped
with a statue of Mercury, sets the stage for the
masterpieces on display in the more than 100
separate galleries.

The National Gallery's permanent collection includes works from the 13th to the 20th century.
A comprehensive survey of Italian paintings and
sculpture includes *The Adoration of the Magi* by
Fra Angelico and Fra Filippo Lippi and *Ginevra
de'Benci*, the only painting by da Vinci outside
of Europe. Flemish and Dutch works, displayed

in a series of attractive panelled rooms, include *Daniel in the Lions' Den*, by Rubens, and a self-portrait by Rembrandt. The Chester Dale Collection comprises works by Impressionist painters such as Degas, Monet, Renoir, and Mary Cassatt.

❻ To get to the **National Gallery of Art's** east building you can take a moving walkway that travels below ground between the two buildings. But to appreciate architect I. M. Pei's impressive, angular east building, enter it from outside rather than from underground. Exit the west building through its eastern doors, and cross 4th Street.

The east building opened in 1978 in response to the changing needs of the National Gallery. While the east building's triangles contrast sharply with the symmetrical classical facade and gentle dome of the west building, both buildings are constructed of pink marble from the same Tennessee quarries. Despite its severe angularity, Pei's building is inviting. The axe-blade–like southwest corner has been darkened and polished smooth by thousands of hands irresistibly drawn to it.

The atrium of the east building is dominated by Alexander Calder's massive mobile, *Untitled*. (It was recently refurbished to make it rotate more easily.) The galleries here generally display modern art, though the east building serves as a home for major temporary exhibitions that span years and artistic styles. *Madison Dr. and 4th St. NW, tel. 202/737–4215. Open Mon.–Sat., 10–5; Sun. 11–6. Extended summer hours are determined annually.*

Time Out Two restaurants on the concourse level between the east and west buildings of the National Gallery offer bleary-eyed and foot-sore museum goers the chance to recharge. The **buffet** serves a wide variety of soups, sandwiches, salads, hot entrees, and desserts. The **Cascade Cafe** has a smaller selection, but customers enjoy the soothing effect of the gentle waterfall that splashes against the glass-covered wall.

Between 7th and 9th streets is the **National Sculpture Garden/Ice Rink** (tel. 202/371–5340).

In the winter skates are rented out for use on the circular rink. Ice cream and other refreshments are available at the green building during the summer.

❼ The **National Museum of Natural History** houses the majority of the Smithsonian's collection of objects, a total of some 118 million specimens. It was constructed in 1910, and two wings were added in the '60s. It is a museum's museum, filled with bones, fossils, stuffed animals, and other natural delights. Exhibits also explore the exploits of humans, the world's most adaptive inhabitants.

The first-floor hall under the rotunda is dominated by a stuffed, eight-ton, 13-foot African bull elephant, one of the largest specimens ever found. (The tusks are fiberglass; the original ivory ones were apparently far too heavy for the stuffed elephant to support.) Off to the right is the popular **Dinosaur Hall.** Fossilized skeletons on display range from a 90-foot-long diplodocus to a tiny thesalosaurus neglectus (a small dinosaur so named because its disconnected bones sat forgotten for years in a college drawer before being reassembled).

In the west wing are displays on birds, mammals, and sea life. Many of the preserved specimens are from the collection of animals bagged by Teddy Roosevelt on his trips to Africa. Not everything in the museum is dead, though. The sea-life display features a living coral reef, complete with fish, plants, and simulated waves. The halls north of the rotunda contain tools, clothing, and other artifacts from many cultures, including those of Native America and of Asia, the Pacific, and Africa. The Discovery Room, in the northwest corner, features elephant tusks, woolly-mammoth teeth, petrified wood, and hundreds of other natural-history objects that visitors can handle and examine.

The highlight of the second floor is the **mineral and gem collection.** Objects include the largest sapphire on public display in the country (the Logan Sapphire, 423 carats), the largest uncut diamond (the Oppenheimer Diamond, 253.7 carats), and, of course, the Hope diamond, a blue gem found in India and reputed to carry a curse.

Also on the second floor is the **Insect Zoo,** popular with children, less so with adults. *Madison Dr. between 9th and 12th Sts. NW, tel. 202/357–2700. Open daily 10–5:30. Extended summer hours determined annually.*

8 The **National Museum of American History**—the next building to the west, toward the Washington Monument—explores America's cultural, political, technical, and scientific past. It opened in 1964 as the National Museum of History and Technology and was renamed in 1980. The incredible diversity of artifacts here helps the Smithsonian live up to its nickname as "the Nation's attic." This is the museum that displayed Muhammed Ali's boxing gloves, the Fonz's leather jacket, and the Bunkers' living room furniture from "All in the Family." Visitors can wander for hours on the museum's three floors. The exhibits on the first floor emphasize the history of science and technology and include such items as farm machines, antique automobiles, early phonographs, and a 280-ton steam locomotive. The second floor is devoted to U.S. social and political history and features an exhibit on everyday American life just after the Revolution. The majority of the first ladies' inaugural gowns are being, in museum parlance, "conserved," a process expected to be completed in 1992. The gowns of the seven most recent first ladies—Jacqueline Kennedy through Barbara Bush—are on display in the second-floor Ceremonial Court, which also features jewels, china, and other artifacts from the White House. The third floor has installations on ceramics, money, graphic arts, musical instruments, photography, and news reporting. The Smithsonian's ample philately collection is scheduled to move from here to a new postal museum on Capitol Hill in 1993. *Madison Ave. between 12th and 14th Sts. NW, tel. 202/357–2700. Open daily 10–5:30.*

To continue the loop of the Mall, head south on 14th Street. From here you'll be able to view the length of the Mall from its western end, this time seeing the Capitol from afar. Instead of turning east on Jefferson Drive, continue south on 14th Street. On the right you'll pass a turreted, castle-like structure called the **Auditor's**

Building. Built in 1879, it was the first building dedicated exclusively to the work of printing America's money. In 1914 the money-making operation was moved one block south to the **Bureau of Engraving and Printing.** All the paper currency in the United States, as well as stamps, military certificates, and presidential invitations, is printed in this huge building. Despite the fact that there are no free samples, the 20-minute, self-guided tour of the Bureau—which takes visitors past presses that turn out some $40 million a day—is one of the city's most popular. *14th and C Sts. SW, tel. 202/447–0193. Open weekdays 9–2.*

Up Independence Avenue, across 12th Street, is the **Freer Gallery of Art,** a gift from Detroit industrialist Charles L. Freer, who retired in 1900 and devoted the rest of his life to collecting Asian treasures. The Freer opened in 1923, four years after its benefactor's death. Nearing the end of an extensive renovation, the Freer is scheduled to reopen in late 1992 or early 1993. Its collection includes more than 26,000 works of art from the Far and Near East, including Asian porcelains, Japanese screens, Chinese paintings and bronzes, and Egyptian gold pieces. Freer's close friend James McNeill Whistler introduced him to Asian art, and the American painter is represented in the vast collection. On display in Gallery 12 is the "Peacock Room," a blue-and-gold dining room decorated with painted leather, wood, and canvas and designed by Whistler for a British shipping magnate. Freer paid $30,000 for the entire room and moved it from London to the United States in 1904.

Just beyond the Freer turn left off of Independence Avenue into the **Enid Haupt Memorial Garden.** This four-acre Victorian-style garden is built largely on the rooftops of the Smithsonian's two newest museums, the Arthur M. Sackler Gallery and the National Museum of African Art, both of which opened in 1987 and sit underground like inverted pyramids.

When Charles Freer endowed the gallery that bears his name, he insisted on a few conditions: objects in the collection could not be loaned out, nor could objects from outside the collections be put on display. Because of these restrictions it was necessary to build a second, complementary, Oriental art museum. The result was the **(11) Arthur M. Sackler Gallery.** A wealthy medical researcher and publisher who began collecting Asian art as a student, Sackler allowed Smithsonian curators to select 1,000 items from his ample collection and pledged $4 million toward the construction of the museum. The collection includes works from China, the Indian subcontinent, Persia, Thailand, and Indonesia. Articles in the permanent collection include Chinese ritual bronzes, jade ornaments from the third millenium BC, Persian manuscripts, and Indian paintings in gold, silver, lapis lazuli, and malachite. *1050 Independence Ave. SW, tel. 202/357–2700. Open daily 10–5:30.*

(12) The other half of the Smithsonian's new underground museum complex is the **National Museum of African Art.** Founded in 1964 as a private educational institution, the museum became part of the Smithsonian in 1979. (Before it was moved here in 1987, the collection was housed in a Capitol Hill townhouse that once belonged to ex-slave Frederick Douglass.) Dedicated to the collection, exhibition, and study of the traditional arts of sub-Saharan Africa, the museum displays artifacts representative of some 900 cultures. The permanent collection includes masks, carvings, textiles, and jewelry, all made from materials such as wood, fiber, bronze, ivory, and fired clay. *950 Independence Ave. SW, tel. 202/357–2700. Open daily 10–5:30.*

You'll find the nearest Metro station, Smithsonian, on Jefferson Drive in front of the Freer Gallery.

Tour 2: The Monuments

Numbers in the margin correspond to points of interest on the Tour 2: The Monuments map.

Washington is a city of monuments. In the middle of traffic circles, on tiny slivers of park, and at street corners and intersections, statues, plaques, and simple blocks of marble honor the generals, politicians, poets, and statesmen who helped shape the nation. The monuments dedicated to the most famous Americans are west of the Mall on ground reclaimed from the marshy flats of the Potomac. This is also the location of Washington's cherry trees, gifts from Japan and focus of a festival each spring.

On this tour we'll walk clockwise among the monuments and through the cherry trees. This can be a leisurely, half-day walk, depending on the speed you travel and the time you spend at each spot. If it's an extremely hot day you may want to hop a Tourmobile bus and travel between the monuments in air-conditioned comfort.

We'll start in front of the tallest of them all, the ❶ **Washington Monument** (nearest Metro stop, Smithsonian). Located at the western end of the Mall, the Washington Monument punctuates the capital like a huge exclamation point. Visible from nearly everywhere in the city, it serves as a landmark for visiting tourists and lost motorists alike.

Congress first authorized a monument to General Washington in 1783. In his 1791 plan for the city, Pierre L'Enfant selected a site (the point where a line drawn west from the Capitol crossed one drawn south from the White House), but it wasn't until 1833, after years of quibbling in Congress, that a private National Monument Society was formed to select a designer and to search for funds. Robert Mills's winning design called for a 600-foot-tall decorated obelisk rising from a circular colonnaded building. The building at the base was to be an American pantheon, adorned with statues of national heroes and a massive statue of Washington riding in a chariot pulled by snorting horses.

Because of the marshy conditions of L'Enfant's original site, the position of the monument was shifted to firmer ground 100 yards southeast. (If you walk a few steps north of the monument you can see the stone marker that denotes L'Enfant's original axis.) The cornerstone was laid in 1848 with the same Masonic trowel Washington himself had used to lay the Capitol's cornerstone 55 years earlier. The Monument Society continued to raise funds after construction was begun, soliciting subscriptions of one dollar from citizens across America. It also

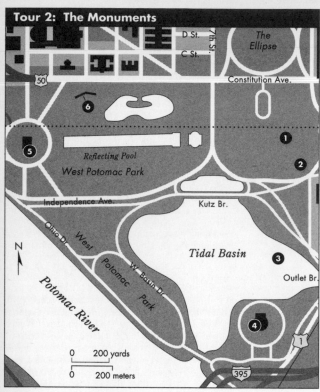

Tour 2: The Monuments

D St.
C St.
7th St.
The Ellipse
Constitution Ave.
6
Reflecting Pool
West Potomac Park
5
1
2
Independence Ave.
Kutz Br.
Ohio Dr.
West
Potomac
Park
W. Basin Dr.
N
Tidal Basin
3
Outlet Br.
Potomac River
4
1
0   200 yards
0   200 meters
395

Jefferson
Memorial, **4**

Lincoln
Memorial, **5**

Sylvan
Theater, **2**

Tidal Basin, **3**

Vietnam
Veterans
Memorial and
Constitution
Gardens, **6**

Washington
Monument, **1**

urged states, organizations, and foreign governments to contribute memorial stones for the construction. A lack of funds and the onset of the Civil War kept the monument at a fraction of its final height, open at the top, and vulnerable to the rain. A clearly visible ring about a third of the way up the obelisk testifies to this unfortunate stage of the monument's history: Although all of the marble in the obelisk came from the same Maryland quarry, that used for the second phase of construction came from a different stratum and is of a slightly different shade.

In 1876 Congress finally appropriated $200,000 to finish the monument, and the Army Corps of Engineers took over construction, simplifying Mill's original design. Work was finally completed in December 1884, when the monument was topped with a 7½-pound piece of aluminum, then one of the most expensive metals in the world. Four years later the monument was opened to visitors, who rode to the top in a steam-operated elevator.

At 555 feet 5 inches, the Washington Monument is the world's tallest masonry structure. The view from the top takes in most of the District and parts of Maryland and Virginia. Visitors are no longer permitted to climb the 898 steps leading to the top. (Incidents of vandalism and a disturbing number of heart attacks on the steps convinced the Park Service that letting people walk up on their own wasn't such a good idea.) On Saturdays there are walk-down tours, with a Park Service guide describing the monument's construction and showing the 193 stone and metal plaques that adorn the inside. *Constitution Ave. at 15th St. NW, tel. 202/426–6840. Open Apr.–Labor Day, daily 8 AM–midnight; Sept.–Mar., daily 9–5.*

After your ascent and descent, walk on the path that leads south from the monument. On your **2** right you'll pass the open-air **Sylvan Theater**, scene of a variety of musical performances during the warmer months. Continue south and cross Independence Avenue at 15th Street. Just south of the red brick **Auditors Building** (the first building constructed by the Federal government to print money) is the site of the **United**

States Holocaust Memorial Museum. Scheduled to open in the spring of 1993, the museum will tell the story of the Jews, Gypsies, Poles, homosexuals, and others who were targeted for death by Nazis between 1933 and 1945. Beyond that is the colonnaded **Bureau of Engraving and Printing.**

3 Carefully cross Maine Avenue at the light and walk down to the **Tidal Basin.** This placid pond was part of the Potomac until 1882, when portions of the river were filled in to improve navigation and create additional parkland, including that upon which the Jefferson Memorial was later built. Paddleboats have been a fixture on the Tidal Basin for years. You can rent one at the boathouse on the east side of the basin, southwest of the Bureau of Engraving. *Northeast bank of Tidal Basin, tel. 202/484-0206. Paddleboat rentals cost $7 an hour, $1.75 each additional quarter hour. Children under 16 must be accompanied by an adult. Open daily 10–6, weather permitting.*

4 Continue down the path that skirts the Tidal Basin and cross the Outlet Bridge to get to the **Jefferson Memorial,** the southernmost of the major monuments in the District. Congress decided that Jefferson deserved a monument positioned as prominently as those in honor of Washington and Lincoln, and this spot directly south of the White House seemed ideal. Jefferson had always admired the Pantheon in Rome—the rotundas he designed for the University of Virginia and his own Monticello were inspired by the dome of the Pantheon—so architect John Russell Pope drew from the same source when he designed this memorial to our third president. Dedicated in 1943, it houses a statue of Jefferson. Its walls are lined with inscriptions based on his writings. One of the best views of the White House can be seen from the memorial's top steps. *Tidal Basin, south bank, tel. 202/426-6821. Open daily 8–midnight.*

After viewing the Jefferson Memorial, continue along the sidewalk that hugs the Tidal Basin. You'll see two grotesque sculpted heads on the sides of the **Inlet Bridge.** The inside walls of the bridge also sport two other interesting sculptures: bronze, human-headed fish that spout water from their mouths. The bridge was refurbished in the 1980s at the same time the chief of the park—a Mr. Jack Fish—was retiring. Sculptor Constantine Sephralis played a little joke: These fish heads are actually Fish's head.

Once you cross the bridge, you have a choice: You can walk to the left, along the Potomac, or continue along the Tidal Basin to the right. The latter route is somewhat more scenic, especially when the cherry trees are in bloom. The first batch of these trees arrived from Japan in 1909. The trees were infected with insects and fungus, however, and the Department of Agriculture ordered them destroyed. A diplomatic crisis was averted when the United States politely asked the Japanese for another batch, and in 1912 Mrs. William Howard Taft planted the first tree. The second was planted by the wife of the Japanese ambassador.

The trees are now the centerpiece of Washington's Cherry Blossom Festival, held each spring. The festivities are kicked off by the lighting of a ceremonial Japanese lantern that rests on the north shore of the Tidal Basin, not far from where the first tree was planted. The once-simple celebration has grown over the years to include concerts, fashion shows, and a parade. Park Service experts try their best to predict exactly when the buds will pop. The trees are usually in bloom for about 10 to 12 days at the beginning of April.

West Potomac Park, the green expanse to the west of the Tidal Basin, is a pleasant place to sit and rest for a while, to watch the paddleboats skim the surface of the Tidal Basin, and to feed the squirrels that usually approach looking for handouts. To get to our next stop, the Lincoln Memorial, walk northwest along West Basin Drive, then cut across to Ohio Drive. Cross Independence Avenue at the light; the traffic here can be dangerous.

5 The **Lincoln Memorial** is considered by many to be the most inspiring monument in the city. It would be hard to imagine Washington without the Lincoln and Jefferson memorials, though they were both criticized when first built. The

Jefferson Memorial was dubbed "Jefferson's muffin"; critics lambasted the design as outdated and too similar to that of the Lincoln Memorial. Some also complained that the Jefferson Memorial blocked the view of the Potomac from the White House. Detractors of the Lincoln Memorial thought it inappropriate that the humble Lincoln be honored with what amounts to a modified but nonetheless rather grandiose Greek temple. The white Colorado-marble memorial was designed by Henry Bacon and completed in 1922. The 36 Doric columns represent the 36 states in the Union at the time of Lincoln's death; the names of the states appear on the frieze above the columns. Above the frieze are the names of the 48 states in the Union when the memorial was dedicated. (Alaska and Hawaii are noted by an inscription on the terrace leading up to the memorial.)

Daniel Chester French's somber statue of the seated president is in the center of the memorial and gazes out over the Reflecting Pool. While French's 19-foot-high sculpture looks as if it were cut from one huge block of stone, it actually comprises 28 interlocking pieces of Georgia marble. Inscribed on the south wall is the Gettysburg Address, and on the north wall is Lincoln's second inaugural address. Above each inscription is a mural painted by Jules Guerin. On the south wall is an angel of truth freeing a slave; the unity of North and South are depicted on the opposite wall. The memorial served as a fitting backdrop for Martin Luther King's "I have a dream" speech in 1963.

Many visitors look only at the front and inside of the Lincoln Memorial, but there is much more to explore. On the lower level to the left is a display that chronicles the memorial's construction. There is also a set of windows that look onto the huge structure's foundation. Stalactites (hanging from above) and stalagmites (growing from below) have formed underneath the marble tribute to Lincoln. Be sure to walk around the marble platform to the rear of the memorial. From there you'll have a clear view over the Arlington Memorial Bridge into Arlington National Cemetery. The Doric-columned Arlington House, once home of General Robert E. Lee, overlooks the cemetery. On a clear night you can see the eternal flame that burns over John F. Kennedy's grave.

Although visiting the area around the Lincoln Memorial during the day allows you to take in an impressive view of the Mall to the east, the best time to see the memorial itself is at night. Spotlights illuminate the outside, while inside, light and shadows play across Lincoln's gentle face. *West end of Mall, tel. 202/426–6895. Open 24 hours a day; staffed daily 8 AM–midnight.*

6 Walk down the steps of the Lincoln Memorial and to the left to get to the **Vietnam Veterans Memorial** and **Constitution Gardens.** The Vietnam Veterans Memorial is another landmark that encourages introspection. The concept came from Jan Scruggs, a former infantry corporal who had served in Vietnam. The stark design of Maya Ying Lin, a 21-year-old Yale architecture student, was selected in a 1981 competition. Upon its completion in 1982, the memorial was decried by some veterans as a "black gash of shame." With the addition of Frederick Hart's statue of three soldiers and a flagpole just south of the Wall, most critics were won over.

The Wall is one of the most visited sites in Washington, its black granite panels reflecting the sky, the trees, and the faces of those looking for the names of friends or relatives who died in the war. The names of more than 58,000 Americans are etched on the face of the memorial in the order of their deaths. Directories at the entrance and exit to the Wall list the names in alphabetical order. (Last year it was discovered that due to a clerical error the names of some two dozen living vets are carved into the stone as well.) For help in finding a specific name, ask a ranger at the blue-and-white hut near the entrance. Thousands of offerings are left at the Wall each year: letters, flowers, medals, uniforms, snapshots. The National Park Service collects these and stores them in a warehouse in Lanham, Maryland, where they are fast becoming another memorial. *Constitution Gardens, 23rd St. and Constitution Ave. NW, tel. 202/634–1568. Open 24 hours a day; staffed 8 AM–midnight.*

Continue east through Constitution Gardens. Veterans groups often have tents set up near the Wall; some provide information on soldiers who remain missing in action, others are on call to help fellow veterans deal with the sometimes powerful emotions that come from visiting the Wall for the first time.

A memorial to veterans of the Korean War is planned for a grove of trees known as Ash Woods near Independence Avenue and the Lincoln Memorial reflecting pool. When completed in 1993, it will consist of a column of American soldiers marching toward a flag pole.

After years of debate over its design and necessity, the Vietnam Womens Memorial—in honor of the women who served in that conflict—is scheduled to be dedicated in 1993. The monument—a bronze figure of a female soldier standing on a marble pad equipped with nozzles that continuously blow a soft mist—sits in Constitution Gardens, southeast of the Vietnam Veterans Memorial.

The FDR, Korean War, and Vietnam Womens memorials have troubled some Washingtonians, who feel the city is entering an unnecessary monument building boom in the 1990s. Each veterans and special interest group seems to want its own separate memorial and there's concern that too many grandiose designs (each group, of course, wants its to be the biggest) are clogging Washington's monumental core.

Time Out At the circular **snack bar** just west of the Constitution Gardens lake you can get hot dogs, potato chips, candy bars, soft drinks, and beer at prices lower than those charged by most street vendors.

The nearest Metro station is Federal Triangle, five blocks to the east on 12th Street.

Tour 3: The White House

Numbers in the margin correspond to points of interest on the Tour 3: The White House Area map.

In a city full of immediately recognizable images, perhaps none is more familiar than the White House. This is where the buck stops and where the nation turns in times of crisis. On this tour we'll visit the White House, then strike out into the surrounding streets to explore the president's neighborhood, which includes some of the oldest houses in the city.

To reach the start of our tour, take the Metro to the McPherson Square station. We'll begin our exploration in front of 1600 Pennsylvania Avenue. Pierre L'Enfant called it the President's House; it was known formally as the Executive Mansion; and in 1902 Congress officially proclaimed it the **White House,** though, contrary to popular belief, it had been given that nickname even before it was painted to cover the fire damage it suffered during the War of 1812. Irishman James Hoban's plan, based on the Georgian design of Leinster Hall near Dublin and of other Irish country homes, was selected in a contest, in 1792. The building wasn't ready for its first occupant until 1800, so George Washington never lived here. Completed in 1829, it has undergone many structural changes since then: Thomas Jefferson, who had entered his own design in the contest under an assumed name, added terraces to the east and west wings. Andrew Jackson installed running water. James Garfield put in the first elevator. Between 1948 and 1952, Harry Truman had the entire structure gutted and restored, adding a second-story porch to the south portico. Each family that has called the White House home has left its imprint on the 132-room mansion. Most recently, George Bush installed a horseshoe pit.

Tuesday through Saturday morning, from 10 AM to noon, selected public rooms on the ground floor and first floor of the White House are open to visitors. Expect a long line, but the wait is worthwhile if you're interested in a firsthand look at what is perhaps the most important building in the city. Most of the year you can simply join the line that forms along the east fence of the White House. Between Memorial Day and Labor Day, however, you'll need tickets to tour the mansion. During the summer months there is a blue-and-green ticket booth

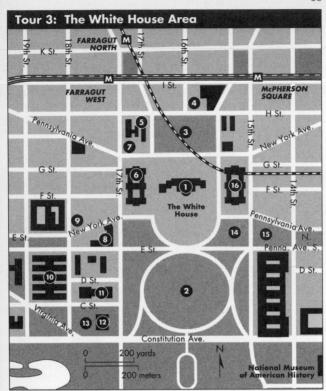

Tour 3: The White House Area

Corcoran Gallery of Art, **8**

Decatur House, **5**

Department of the Interior, **10**

Ellipse, **2**

House of the Americas, **12**

Lafayette Square, **3**

Memorial Continental Hall, **11**

Museum of Modern Art of Latin America, **13**

Octagon House, **9**

Old Executive Office Building, **6**

Pershing Park, **15**

Renwick Gallery, **7**

St. John's Episcopal Church, **4**

Treasury Building, **16**

White House, **1**

William Tecumseh Sherman Monument, **14**

② on the **Ellipse** just south of the White House, open between 8 AM and noon, Tuesday through Saturday, dispensing tickets on a first-come, first-served basis. (Tickets are often gone by 9 AM.) Your ticket will show the approximate time of your tour. There is seating on the Ellipse for those waiting to see the White House. Volunteer marching bands, drill teams, and other musical groups usually perform here, entertaining those who are stuck in line. If you write your representative or senator's office well in advance of your trip, you can receive special VIP passes for tours between 8 and 10 AM. On selected weekends in April and October, the White House is open for garden tours. In December it's decorated for the holidays.

You'll enter the White House through the East Wing lobby on the ground floor, walking past the Jacqueline Kennedy Rose Garden. Your first stop is the large white-and-gold **East Room,** the site of presidential news conferences. In 1814 Dolley Madison saved the room's full-length portrait of George Washington from torch-carrying British soldiers by cutting it from its frame, rolling it up, and spiriting it out of the White House. (No fool she, Dolley also rescued her own portrait.) A later occupant, Teddy Roosevelt, allowed his children to ride their pet pony in the East Room.

The Federal-style **Green Room,** named for the moss-green watered silk that covers its walls, is used for informal receptions and "photo opportunities" with foreign heads of state. Notable furnishings in this room include a New England sofa that once belonged to Daniel Webster and portraits of Benjamin Franklin, John Quincy Adams, and Abigail Adams.

The elliptical **Blue Room,** the most formal space in the White House, is furnished with a gilded Empire-style settee and chairs that were ordered by James Monroe. (Monroe asked for plain wooden chairs, but the furniture manufacturer thought such unadorned furnishings too simple for the White House and took it upon himself to supply chairs more in keeping with their surroundings.) The White House Christmas tree is placed in this room each year. Another well-known elliptical room, the president's **Oval Office,** is in the semidetached West Wing of the White House, along with other executive offices.

The **Red Room** is decorated as an American Empire–style parlor of the early 19th century, with furniture by the New York cabinetmaker Charles-Honoré Lannuier. You'll recognize the marble mantel as the twin of the mantel in the Green Room.

The **State Dining Room,** second in size only to the East Room, can seat 140 guests. The room is dominated by G.P.A. Healy's portrait of Abraham Lincoln, painted after the president's death. The stone mantel is inscribed with a quotation from one of John Adams's letters: "I pray heaven to bestow the best of blessings on this house and all that shall hereafter inhabit it. May none but honest and wise men ever rule under this roof." In Teddy Roosevelt's day a stuffed moose head hung over the mantel. *1600 Pennsylvania Ave. NW, tel. 202/456–7041 (recorded information) or 202/472–3669. Open Tues.–Sat. 10 AM–noon.*

❸ **Lafayette Square,** bordered by Pennsylvania Avenue, Madison Place, H Street, and Jackson Place, is an intimate oasis in the midst of downtown Washington. With such an important resident living across the street, National Capital Park Service gardeners lavish extra attention on the square's trees and flower beds.

When Pierre L'Enfant proposed the location for the Executive Mansion, the only building north of what is today Pennsylvania Avenue was the Pierce family farmhouse, which stood at the northeast corner of what is today Lafayette Square. An apple orchard and a family burial ground were the area's two other main features. During the construction of the White House, workers' huts and a brick kiln were set up, and soon private residences began popping up around the square (though sheep would continue to graze on it for years). L'Enfant's original plan for the city designated this area as part of "President's Park"; in essence it was the president's front yard, just as what is now the Ellipse was once his backyard. The egalitarian Thomas

Jefferson, concerned that large, landscaped White House grounds would give the wrong impression in a democratic country, ordered that the area be turned into a public park. Soldiers camped in the square during the War of 1812 and the Civil War, turning it at both times into a muddy pit. Today, protesters set their placards up in Lafayette Square, jockeying for positions that face the White House. While the National Park Service can't restrict the protesters' freedom of speech, it does try to restrict the size of their signs.

Standing in the center of the park—and dominating the square—is a large **statue of Andrew Jackson.** Erected in 1853 and cast from bronze cannon that Jackson had captured during the War of 1812, this was the first equestrian statue made in America. (An exact duplicate faces St. Louis Cathedral in New Orleans' Jackson Square.)

Jackson's is the only statue of an American in the park. The other statues are of foreign-born soldiers who helped in America's fight for independence. In the southeast corner is the park's namesake, the **Marquis de Lafayette,** the young French nobleman who came to America to fight in the Revolution. When Lafayette returned to the United States in 1824 he was given a rousing welcome: He was wined and dined in the finest homes and showered with gifts of cash and land. (You can imagine how this must have made his countryman Pierre L'Enfant feel. The designer of the city Lafayette took by storm had by that time been forgotten.)

If you head east on H Street for half a block, you'll come to the **United States Government Bookstore** (1510 H St. NW, tel. 202/653–5075), the place to visit if you'd like to buy a few pounds of the millions of tons of paper the government churns out each year. Here is where you'll find a copy of the latest Federal budget or *The Surgeon General's Report on Nutrition and Health.*

Time Out   Presidential advisor Bernard Baruch used to eat his lunch in Lafayette Park, and you can too. **Loeb's Restaurant** (around the corner at 15th and I streets NW) is a New York–style deli that serves up salads and sandwiches to eat there or to go.

❹ On H Street is the golden-domed **St. John's Episcopal Church,** the so-called "Church of the Presidents." Every president since Madison has visited the church, and many worshipped here on a regular basis. Built in 1816, the church was the second building on the square. Benjamin Latrobe, who worked on both the Capitol and the White House, designed it in the form of a Greek cross, with a flat dome and a lantern cupola. The church has been altered somewhat since then; later additions include the Doric portico and the cupola tower. You can best sense the intent of Latrobe's design while standing inside under the saucer-shaped dome of the original building. Not far from the center of the church is pew 54, where visiting presidents are seated. Brochures are available inside for those who would like to take a self-guided tour. *16th and H Sts. NW, tel. 202/347–8766. Open Mon.–Sat. 8–4. Tours after 11 AM Sun. service and by appointment.*

❺ The redbrick, Federal-style **Decatur House** on the corner of H Street and Jackson Place was the first private residence on President's Park (the White House doesn't really count as *private*). Designed by Benjamin Latrobe, the house was built for naval hero Stephen Decatur and his wife Susan in 1819. Decatur had earned the affection of the nation in battles against the British and the Barbary pirates. Planning to start a political career, he used the prize money Congress awarded him for his exploits to build this home near the White House. Tragically, only 14 months after he moved in, Decatur was killed in a duel with James Barron, a disgruntled former Navy officer who held Decatur responsible for his court-martial. Later occupants of the house included Henry Clay, Martin Van Buren, and the Beales, a prominent family from the West whose modifications of the building include a parquet floor showing the state seal of California. The house is now operated by the National Trust. The first floor is furnished as it was in Decatur's time. The second floor is furnished in the Victorian style favored by the Beale family, who owned it until 1956 (thus making Decatur House both the first and *last* private residence on Lafayette Square). The National Trust store around the corner (entrance on H Street) sells a variety of books, postcards, and gifts. *748 Jackson Place NW, tel. 202/842–0920. Open Tues.–Fri. 10–2, weekends noon–4. Admission: $3 adults, $1.50 senior citizens and students under 18, free to children under 5 and National Trust members. Tours on the hour and half hour.*

Directly across Pennsylvania Avenue, to the right of the White House, is the **Old Executive Office Building,** which has gone from being one of the most detested buildings in the city to one of the most beloved. It was built between 1871 and 1888 and originally housed the War, Navy, and State departments. Its architect, Alfred B. Mullett, patterned it after the Louvre, but detractors quickly criticized the busy French Empire design—with its mansard roof, tall chimneys, and 900 freestanding columns—as an inappropriate counterpoint to the Greek Revival Treasury Building that sits on the other side of the White House. Numerous plans to alter the facade foundered due to lack of money. The granite edifice may look like a wedding cake, but its high ceilings and spacious offices make it popular with occupants, who currently include the vice president, the Office of Management and Budget, the National Security Council, and other agencies of the executive branch.

Continue west on Pennsylvania Avenue. At the end of the block, with the motto "Dedicated to Art" engraved above the entrance, is the **Renwick Gallery.** The French Second Empire–style building was designed by Smithsonian Castle architect James Renwick in 1859 to house the art collection of Washington merchant and banker William Wilson Corcoran, founder of Riggs Bank. Corcoran was a Southern sympathizer who spent the duration of the Civil War in Europe. While he was away his unfinished building was pressed into service by the government as a Quartermaster's General post. When the Corcoran finally opened in 1874 it was the first private art museum in the city. The gallery's Grand Salon at the top of the central stairway was furnished in an opulent Vic-

torian style, with paintings hung in tiers, one
atop the other. (In the background of Corcoran's portrait is the Renwick itself.) The Octagon Room, at the front of the second floor, was
built to display Hiram Powers's sculpture *The
Greek Slave*. The statue—a nude woman with
her wrists chained—was considered so shock-
ing that separate viewing hours were established for men and women, and children under
16 were not allowed to see it at all. Corcoran's
collection quickly outgrew the building and in
1897 was moved to a new gallery a few blocks
south on 17th Street (described below). After a
stint as the U.S. Court of Claims, this building
was restored to its former glory, renamed after
its architect, and opened as the Smithsonian's
museum of American decorative arts in 1972.
The collection covers a wide range of disciplines
and styles; special exhibits have included such
items as blown glass, Shaker furniture, and contemporary crafts. *Pennsylvania Ave. and 17th
St. NW, tel. 202/357-2700. Open daily 10-5:30.*

8 Head south on 17th Street. At the corner of 17th
Street and New York Avenue is the **Corcoran
Gallery of Art,** one of the few large museums in
Washington outside the Smithsonian family.
The Beaux Arts–style building, its copper roof
green with age, was designed by Ernest Flagg
and completed in 1897. The gallery's permanent
collection numbers more than 11,000 works, including paintings by the first great American
portraitists John Copley, Gilbert Stuart, and
Rembrandt Peale. The Hudson River School is
represented by such works as *Mount Corcoran*
by Albert Bierstadt and Frederic Church's *Ni-
agara*. There are also portraits by Sargent,
Eakins, and Mary Cassatt. European artwork is
included in the Walker Collection (late 19th- and
early 20th-century paintings, including works
by Gustave Courbet, Monet, Pissarro, and Renoir) and the Clark Collection (Dutch, Flemish,
and French Romantic paintings, and the recently restored entire 18th-century Grand Salon of
the Hotel d'Orsay in Paris). Also be sure to see
Samuel Morse's *The Old House of Representatives* and Hiram Powers's *The Greek Slave*,
which scandalized Victorian society. The adja-
cent Corcoran School is the only four-year art

college in the Washington area. *17th St. and
New York Ave. NW, tel. 202/638–1439 (record-
ing), 202/638–3211. Open Tues.–Sun. 10–4:30,
Thurs. 10–9. Closed Mon., Christmas, and New
Year's Day. Suggested donation: $3 adults, $2
students and senior citizens.*

9 A block up New York Avenue, at the corner of
18th Street, is the **Octagon House,** built in 1801
for John Tayloe III, a wealthy Virginia plantation owner. Designed by William Thornton, the
Octagon House actually has only six sides, not
eight. Thornton chose the unusual shape to conform to the acute angle formed by L'Enfant's intersection of New York Avenue and 18th Street.

After the White House was burned in 1814, the
Tayloes invited James and Dolley Madison to
stay in the Octagon House. It was in a second-
floor study that the Treaty of Ghent, ending the
War of 1812, was signed. By the late 1800s the
building was used as a rooming house. In this
century the house served as the headquarters of
the American Institute of Architects before the
construction of AIA's rather unexceptional
building behind it. In the '60s, Octagon House
was restored to its former splendor, with de-
tailed plaster molding around the ceilings, coal-
burning stoves in the entryway, and the original
1799 Coade stone mantels (made using a now-
lost method of casting crushed stone). Exhibits
relating to architecture, decorative arts, and
Washington history are mounted in the upstairs
galleries. *1799 New York Ave. NW, tel. 202/638–
3105. Open Tues.–Fri. 10–4, weekends noon–4.
Closed Christmas and New Year's Day. Suggested donation: $2 adults, $1.50 senior citizens, $1 children.*

10 A block south on 18th Street is the **Department
of the Interior** building, designed by Waddy B.
Wood. At the time of its construction in 1937 it
was the most modern federal building in the city
and the first with escalators and central air-con-
ditioning. While the outside of the building is
somewhat plain, much of the interior is decorated with paintings that reflect the Interior
Department's work. Hallways feature heroic oil
paintings of dam construction, panning for gold,
and cattle drives. You'll pass some of these if you

visit the **Department of the Interior Museum** on
the first floor. (You can enter the building at its
E Street or C Street doors; adults must show
photo ID.) Soon after it opened in 1938, the museum became one of the most popular attractions in Washington; evening hours were
maintained even during the Second World War.
While some of the displays seem a bit dated—
such as one that outlines "vital products derived
from the range," including clock cords, emery
cloth, hat sweatbands, and isinglass—this snap-
shot from the '30s is a welcome contrast to the
high-tech, interactive video museums of today.
Especially appealing are the meticulously created dioramas depicting various historical
events and American locales, including a 1938
animated scene of Juneau, Alaska, complete
with tiny train cars moving on a track. The Indian Craft Shop across the hall from the museum
sells Native American pottery, dolls, carvings,
jewelry, baskets, and books. It, too, has been
part of the Department of the Interior since
1938. *C and E Sts. between 18th and 19th Sts.
NW, tel. 202/208-4743. Open weekdays 8-4.*

① A block south is **Memorial Continental Hall,**
headquarters of the Daughters of the American Revolution. This Beaux Arts building was
the site each year of the D.A.R.'s congress until the larger Constitution Hall was built around
the corner. An entrance on D Street leads to the
D.A.R. Museum. Its 50,000-item collection includes fine examples of Colonial and Federal silver, china, porcelain, stoneware, earthenware,
and glass. Thirty-three period rooms are decorated in styles representative of various U.S.
states, ranging from an 1850 California adobe
parlor to a New Hampshire attic filled with toys
from the 18th and 19th centuries. *1776 D St.
NW, tel. 202/879-3240. Open weekdays 8:30-4,
Sun. 1-5. Docents available for tours weekdays
10-2:30.*

⑫ Just across C Street to the south of Continental
Hall is the **House of the Americas,** the headquarters building of the Organization of American
States. The interior of this building features a
cool patio adorned with a pre-Columbian–style
fountain and lush tropical plants. This tiny rain
forest is a good place to rest when Washington's

summer heat is at its most oppressive. The upstairs Hall of Flags and Heroes contains, as the
name implies, busts of generals and statesmen
from the various OAS member countries as well
as each country's flag. *17th St. and Constitution
Ave. NW, tel. 202/458–3000. Open weekdays 9–
5:30.*

Behind the House of the Americas is the
13 **Museum of Modern Art of Latin America,** with
its entrance on 18th Street. The small gallery—
the world's first devoted to art of this region—is
in a building that formerly served as the residence for the secretary general of the OAS. *201
18th St. NW, tel. 202/458–6016. Open Tues.–
Sat. 10–5.*

Next, head east on Constitution Avenue and
take the first left, following the curving drive
that encircles the Ellipse.

The **Ellipse** is bounded by Constitution Avenue,
E Street, 15th Street, and 17th Street. From
this vantage point you can see the Washington
Monument and the Jefferson Memorial to the
south and the red-tile roof of the Department of
Commerce to the east, with the tower of the Old
Post Office Building sticking up above it. To the
north you have a good view of the back of the
White House; the rounded portico and Harry
Truman's second-story porch are clearly visible. The south lawn of the White House serves
as a heliport for "Marine One," the president's
helicopter. Each Monday after Easter the south
lawn is also the scene of the White House Easter
Egg Roll. The **National Christmas Tree** grows on
the northern edge of the Ellipse. Each year in
late November it is lighted by the president during a festive ceremony that marks the beginning
of the holiday season.

Across E Street to the northeast of the Ellipse,
in a small park bounded by E Street, 15th
Street, Treasury Place, and South Executive
14 Place, stands the massive **William Tecumseh
Sherman Monument.** Just north of this memorial is the southern facade of the Treasury
Building, its entrance guarded by a **statue of
Alexander Hamilton,** the department's first
secretary.

⑮ Across 15th Street to the east is **Pershing Park,** a quiet, sunken garden that honors General "Blackjack" Pershing, commander of the American expeditionary force in World War I. Engravings on the stone walls recount pivotal campaigns from that war. Ice skaters glide on the square pool in the winter.

One block to the north is the venerable **Hotel Washington** (515 15th St., tel. 202/638–5900). Its lobby is narrow and unassuming, but the view from the rooftop Sky Top Lounge—open May to October—is one of the best in the city.

⑯ To your left is the long side of the **Treasury Building,** the largest Greek Revival edifice in Washington. Pierre L'Enfant had intended for Pennsylvania Avenue to stretch in a straight, unbroken line from the White House to the Capitol. This plan was ruined by the construction of the Treasury building on this site just east of the White House. Designed by Robert Mills, the Treasury was constructed between 1836 and 1851.

Time Out A glittering urban mall, **The Shops** (in the National Press Building, F and G Sts. between 13th and 14th Sts. NW) is home to table-service restaurants such as the **American Cafe** and the **Boston Seafood Company,** as well as faster and cheaper fare in its top-floor Food Hall.

Continue up 15th Street. The luxurious **Old Ebbitt Grill** (675 15th St. NW, tel. 202/347–4800) is a popular watering spot for journalists and television news correspondents.

The Metro stations nearest to the end of this tour are McPherson Square, two blocks north to 15th Street and a block to the west on I Street, and Metro Center, three blocks east on G Street.

Tour 4: Capitol Hill

Numbers in the margin correspond to points of interest on the Tour 4: Capitol Hill map.

The people who live and work on "the Hill" do so in the shadow of the edifice that lends the neighborhood its name: the gleaming white Capitol building. More than just the center of government, however, the Hill also includes charming residential blocks lined with Victorian row houses and a fine assortment of restaurants, bars, and shops. Capitol Hill's boundaries are disputed: It's bordered to the west, north, and south by the Capitol, Union Station, and I Street respectively. Some argue that Capitol Hill extends east to the Anacostia River, others that it ends at 11th Street near Lincoln Park. The neighborhood does in fact seem to grow as members of Capitol Hill's active historic-preservation movement restore more and more 19th-century houses.

❶ Start your exploration of the Hill inside the cavernous main hall of **Union Station,** which sits on Massachusetts Avenue north of the Capitol. In 1902 the McMillan Commission—charged with suggesting ways to improve the appearance of the city—recommended that the many train lines that sliced through the capital share one main depot. Union Station was opened in 1908 and was the first building completed under the Commission's plan. Chicago architect and commission member Daniel H. Burnham patterned the station after the Roman Baths of Diocletian.

For many visitors to Washington, the capital city is first seen framed through the grand station's arched doorways. In its heyday, during World War II, more than 200,000 people swarmed through the station daily. By the '60s, however, the decline in train travel had turned the station into an expensive white-marble elephant. It was briefly, and unsuccessfully, transformed into a visitors center for the Bicentennial; but by 1981 rain was pouring in through the neglected station's roof, and passengers boarded trains at a ramshackle depot behind the station.

The Union Station you see today is the result of a restoration completed in 1988, an effort intended to be the beginning of a revival of Washington's east end. It's hoped the shops, restaurants, and nine-screen movie theater in Union Station will draw more than just train travelers to the Beaux Arts building. The jewel of the structure remains its meticulously re-

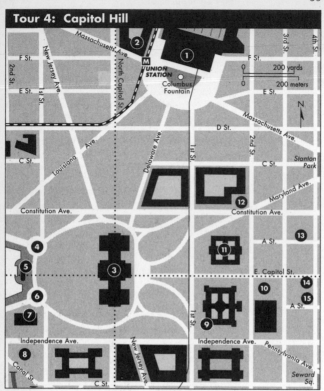

Tour 4: Capitol Hill

Bartholdi
Fountain, **8**

Capitol, **3**

City Post
Office, **2**

Folger
Shakespeare
Library, **10**

Frederick
Douglass
Townhouse, **13**

Grant
Memorial, **5**

James Garfield
Memorial, **6**

Library of
Congress, **9**

Peace
Monument, **4**

Sewall-Belmont
House, **12**

South side of
East Capitol
Street, **14**

Supreme Court
Building, **11**

326 A Street, **15**

Union Station, **1**

United States
Botanic
Gardens, **7**

stored main waiting room. With its 96-foot-high coffered ceiling gilded with eight pounds of gold leaf, it is one of the city's great spaces and is used for inaugural balls and other festive events. Forty-six statues of Roman legionnaires, one for each state in the Union when the station was completed, ring the grand room. The statues were the subject of controversy when the building was first opened. Pennsylvania Railroad president Alexander Cassatt (brother of artist Mary) ordered sculptor Louis Saint-Gaudens to alter the statues, convinced that the legionnaires' skimpy outfits would scandalize female passengers. The sculptor obligingly added a shield to each figure, obscuring any offending body parts.

The east hall, now filled with vendors, was once an expensive restaurant. It is decorated with Pompeiian tracery and plaster walls and columns painted to look like marble. At one time the station also featured a secure presidential waiting room, now the Adirondacks Restaurant. The private waiting room was by no means a frivolous addition: Twenty years before Union Station was built, President Garfield was assassinated in the public waiting room of the old Baltimore and Potomac terminal on 6th Street. Group tours available by appointment (tel. 202/289–1908).

Time Out   On Union Station's lower level you'll find more than 20 food stalls, offering everything from pizza to sushi. On the main level are Capitol Hill favorite the **American Cafe,** the trendy Italian restaurant **Sfuzzi,** and **America,** which offers a menu as expansive as its name: everything from Albuquerque blue corn enchiladas to New York Reuben sandwiches.

As you walk out Union Station's front doors, glance to the right. At the end of a long succession of archways is the Washington **City Post Office,** also designed by Daniel Burnham and completed in 1914. Nostalgic odes to the noble mail carrier are inscribed on the exterior of the marble building; one of them characterizes the mailman as "Messenger of sympathy and love, servant of parted friends, consoler of the lonely, bond of the scattered family, enlarger of the common life." The Post Office is currently being renovated, scheduled to open in late 1993 as the **National Postal History and Philatelic Museum,** the 14th Smithsonian museum in Washington. The $15.4 million museum will contain rare stamps now in the National Museum of American History as well as exhibits on postal history and transportation.

Return to Union Station and walk to the plaza in front. At the center of the plaza is the **Columbus Memorial Fountain,** designed by Lorado Taft. A caped, steely-eyed Christopher Columbus stares into the distance, flanked by a hoary, bearded figure (the Old World) and an Indian brave (the New).

Head south from the fountain, away from Union Station, cross Massachusetts Avenue, and walk down Delaware Avenue.

❸ Cross Constitution Avenue and enter the **Capitol** grounds, landscaped in the late-19th century by Frederick Law Olmsted, Sr., who, along with Calvert Vaux, created New York City's Central Park. On these 68 acres you will find both the tamest squirrels in the city and the highest concentration of television news correspondents, jockeying for a good position in front of the Capitol for their "stand-ups."

When planning the city, Pierre L'Enfant described the gentle rise on which the Capitol sits, known then as Jenkins Hill, as "a pedestal waiting for a monument." The design of this monument was the result of a competition held in 1792; the winner was William Thornton, a physician and amateur architect from the West Indies. With its central rotunda and dome, Thornton's Capitol is reminiscent of Rome's Pantheon, a similarity that must have delighted the Nation's founders, who felt the American government was based on the principles of the Republic of Rome.

The cornerstone was laid by George Washington in a Masonic ceremony on September 18, 1793, and in November 1800, both the Senate and the House of Representatives moved down from Philadelphia to occupy the first completed section of the Capitol: the boxlike portion between the central rotunda and today's north wing. By 1806 the House wing had been completed, just to the south of what is now the domed center, and a covered wooden walkway joined the two wings.

The Congress House grew slowly and suffered a grave setback on August 24, 1814, when British troops led by Sir George Cockburn marched on Washington and set fire to the Capitol and numerous other government buildings. The wooden walkway was destroyed and the two wings gutted, but the walls were left standing after a violent rainstorm doused the flames. Fearful that Congress might leave Washington, residents raised money for a hastily built "Brick Capitol" that stood where the Supreme Court is today. Architect Benjamin Henry Latrobe supervised the rebuilding of the Capitol, adding such American touches as the corn-cob-and-tobacco-leaf capitals to columns in the east entrance to the Senate wing. He was followed by Boston-born Charles Bulfinch, and in 1826 the Capitol, its low wooden dome sheathed in copper, was finally finished.

North and south wings were added in the 1850s and '60s to accommodate a growing government trying to keep pace with a growing country. The elongated edifice extended farther north and south than Thornton had planned, and in 1855, to keep the scale correct, work began on a tall cast-iron dome. President Lincoln was criticized for continuing this expensive project while the country was in the throes of the bloody Civil War, but he called the construction "a sign we intend the Union shall go on." This twin-shelled dome, a marvel of 19th-century engineering, rises 285 feet above the ground and weighs 9 million pounds. It expands and contracts up to four inches a day, depending on the outside temperature. The figure on top of the dome, often mistaken for Pocahontas, is called *Freedom*. Sculptor Thomas Crawford had first planned for the 19-foot-tall bronze statue to wear the cloth liberty cap of a freed Roman slave, but southern lawmakers, led by Jefferson Davis, objected. An "American" headdress composed of a star-encircled helmet surmounted with an eagle's head and feathers was substituted.

Guided tours of the Capitol usually start beneath the dome in the Rotunda, but if there's a crowd you may have to wait in a line that forms at the top of the center steps on the east side. If you want to forgo the tour, which is brief but informative, you may look around on your own. Enter through one of the lower doors to the right or left of the main steps. Start your exploration under Constantino Brumidi's *Apotheosis of Washington*, the fresco in the center of the dome. Working as Michelangelo did in the Sistine Chapel, applying paint to wet plaster, Brumidi completed this fresco in 1865. The figures in the inner circle represent the 13 original states of the Union; those in the outer ring symbolize arts, sciences, and industry. The flat, sculpture-style frieze around the rim of the Rotunda depicting 400 years of American history was started by Brumidi. While painting Penn's treaty with the Indians, the 74-year-old artist slipped on the 58-foot-high scaffold and almost fell off. Brumidi managed to hang on until help arrived, but he died a few months later from shock brought on by the incident. The work was continued by another Italian, Filippo Costaggini, but the frieze wasn't finished until American Allyn Cox added the final touches in 1953.

South of the Rotunda is Statuary Hall, once the legislative chamber of the House of Representatives. The room has an interesting architectural feature that maddened early legislators: A slight whisper uttered on one side of the hall can be heard on the other. (Don't be disappointed if this parlor trick doesn't work when you're visiting the Capitol; sometimes the hall is just too noisy.) When the House moved out, Congress invited each state to send statues of two great deceased citizens for placement in the former chamber. Because the weight of the accumulated statues threatened to cave the floor in, some of the sculptures were dispersed to various other spots throughout the Capitol.

To the north, on the Senate side, you can visit the chamber once used by the Supreme Court as well as the splendid Old Senate Chamber, both of which have been restored. Also be sure to see the Brumidi Corridor on the ground floor of the senate wing. Frescoes and oil paintings of birds, plants, and American inventions adorn the walls and ceilings, and an intricate, Brumidi-designed bronze stairway leads to the second floor. The Italian artist also memorialized several American heroes, painting them inside trompe l'oeil frames. Trusting that America would continue to produce heroes long after he was gone, Brumidi left some frames empty. The most recent one to be filled, in 1987, honors the crew of the space shuttle Challenger.

If you want to watch some of the legislative action in the **House** or **Senate chambers** while you're on the Hill you'll have to get a gallery pass from the office of your representative or senator. (To find out where those offices are, ask any Capitol police officer, or dial 202/224–3121.) In the chambers you'll notice that Democrats sit to the right of the presiding officer, Republicans to the left—the opposite, it's often noted, of their political leanings. You may be disappointed by watching from the gallery. Most of the day-to-day business is conducted in the various legislative committees, many of which meet in the Congressional office buildings. The *Washington Post*'s daily "Today in Congress" lists when and where the committees are meeting. To get to a house or senate office building, go to the Capitol's basement and ride the miniature subway used by legislators. *East end of the Mall, tel. 202/224–3121. For guide service, tel. 202/225–6827. Open daily 9–4:30; summer hours determined annually.*

Time Out A meal at a **Capitol cafeteria** may give you a glimpse of a well-known politician or two. A public dining room on the first floor, Senate-side, is open from 7:30 AM to 4:30 PM when Congress is in session, 7:30 to 3:30 at other times. A favorite with legislators is the Senate bean soup, made and served everyday since 1901 (no one is sure exactly why, though the menu, which you can take with you, outlines a few popular theories).

When you're finished exploring the inside of the Capitol, make your way to the west side. In 1981,

Ronald Reagan broke with tradition and moved the presidential swearing-in ceremony to this side of the Capitol, which offers a dramatic view of the Mall and monuments below and can accommodate more guests than the east side, where all previous presidents took the oath of office. Walk down the northernmost flight of steps and follow the red-and-black path that leads to Pennsylvania Avenue. The white-marble memorial in the center of the traffic circle in

❹ front of you is the **Peace Monument**, which depicts America, grief-stricken over sailors lost at sea, weeping on the shoulder of History. Cross First Street carefully and walk to the left along the **Capitol Reflecting Pool.** As you continue

❺ south you'll pass the **Grant Memorial.** At a length of 252 feet, it's the largest sculpture group in the city. The statue of Ulysses S. Grant on horseback is flanked by Union artillery and cavalry. Further south, in the intersection of First Street and Maryland Avenue SW, is the

❻ **James Garfield Memorial.** The 20th president of the United States, Garfield was assassinated in 1881 after only a few months in office.

❼ Across Maryland Avenue is the **United States Botanic Gardens,** a peaceful, plant-filled oasis between Capitol Hill and the Mall. The conservatory includes a cactus house, a fern house, and a subtropical house filled with orchids. Seasonal displays include blooming plants at Easter, chrysanthemums in the fall, and Christmas greens and poinsettias in December and January. Brochures just inside the doorway offer helpful gardening tips. *1st St. and Maryland Ave. SW, tel. 202/225–8333. Open June–Aug., daily 9–9; Sept.–May, daily 9–5.*

Walk east on Independence Avenue. On the right, in a park that is part of the Botanic Gar-

❽ den, you'll pass the **Bartholdi Fountain.** Frédéric-Auguste Bartholdi, sculptor of the more famous—and much larger—Statue of Liberty, created this delightful fountain for the Philadelphia Centennial Exhibition of 1876. With its aquatic monsters, sea nymphs, tritons, and lighted globes (once gas, now electric), the fountain represents the elements of water and light.

Cross 1st Street SW and continue east on Independence Avenue past the **Rayburn, Longworth,** and **Cannon House office buildings.** At Independence Avenue and 1st Street SE is the green-domed **Jefferson Building** of the **Library of Congress.** Like many buildings in Washington that seem a bit overwrought (the Old Executive Office Building is another example), the library was criticized when it was completed, in 1897. Some detractors felt its Italian-Renaissance design was a bit too florid. Congressmen were even heard to grumble that its dome competed with that of their Capitol. It is certainly decorative, with busts of Dante, Goethe, Hawthorne, and other great writers perched above its entryway. *The Court of Neptune,* Roland Hinton Perry's fountain at the base of the front steps, rivals some of Rome's best fountains.

Provisions for a library to serve members of Congress were originally made in 1800, when the government set aside $5,000 to purchase and house books that legislators might need to consult. This small collection was housed in the Capitol but was destroyed in 1814, when the British burned the city. Thomas Jefferson, then in retirement at Monticello, offered his personal library as a replacement, noting that "there is, in fact, no subject to which a Member of Congress may not have occasion to refer." Jefferson's collection of 6,487 books, for which Congress eventually paid him $23,950, laid the foundation for the great national library. (Sadly, another fire in 1851 wiped out two-thirds of Jefferson's books.) By the late 1800s it was clear the Capitol building could no longer contain the growing library, and the Jefferson Building was constructed. The **Adams Building,** on 2nd Street behind the Jefferson, was added in 1939. A third structure, the **James Madison Building,** was opened in 1980; it is just south of the Jefferson Building, between Independence Avenue and C Street.

The **Library of Congress** today holds some 90 million items, of which 30 million are books. Also part of the library is the Congressional Research Service, which, as the name implies, works on special projects for senators and representatives.

The Jefferson and Adams buildings are nearing the end of an extensive renovation and some parts may be closed on your visit. Recently reopened in the Jefferson Building, however, is the grand, octagonal Main Reading Room, its central desk surrounded by mahogany reader's tables. Computer terminals have replaced the wooden card catalogs, but books are still retrieved and disbursed the same way: Readers (18 years or older) hand request slips to librarians and wait patiently for their materials to be delivered. Researchers aren't allowed in the stacks and only members of Congress can check books out.

But books are only part of the story. Family trees are explored in the Local History and Genealogy Reading Room. In the Folklife Reading Room, patrons can listen to LP recordings of American Indian music or hear the story of B'rer Rabbit read in the Gullah dialect of Georgia and South Carolina. Items from the library's collection—which includes a Gutenberg bible—are often on display in the Jefferson and Madison buildings. Classic films are shown for free in the 64-seat Mary Pickford Theater (tel. 202/707–5677 for information). *Jefferson Building, 1st St. and Independence Ave. SE, tel. 202/707–5458. Open weekdays 8:30–9:30, weekends 8:30–6.*

⓵ Behind the Jefferson Building stands the **Folger Shakespeare Library.** The Folger Library's collection of works by and about Shakespeare and his times is second to none. The white-marble Art Deco building, designed by architect Paul Philippe Cret, is decorated with scenes from the Bard's plays. Inside is a reproduction of an inn-yard theater that is home to the acclaimed Shakespeare Theatre at the Folger. A gallery, designed in the manner of an Elizabethan Great Hall, hosts rotating exhibits from the library's collection. *201 E. Capitol St. SE, tel. 202/544–4600. Open Mon.–Sat. 10–4.*

⓫ Walk back down East Capitol Street and turn right onto 1st Street. The stolid **Supreme Court Building** faces 1st Street here. The justices arrived in Washington in 1800 along with the rest of the government but were for years shunted around various rooms in the Capitol; for a while they even met in a tavern. It wasn't until 1935 that the Court got its own building, this white-marble temple with twin rows of Corinthian columns, designed by Cass Gilbert. William Howard Taft, the only man to serve as both president and chief justice, was instrumental in getting the court a home of its own, though he died before it was completed.

The Supreme Court convenes on the first Monday in October and remains in session until it has heard all of its cases and handed down all its decisions (usually the end of July). For two weeks of each month (Monday through Wednesday), the justices hear oral arguments in the velvet-swathed court chamber. Visitors who want to listen can choose from two lines. One is a "three-to five-minute" line, which shuttles visitors through, giving them a quick impression of the court at work. The other is for those who'd like to stay for the whole show. If you choose the latter, it's best to be in line by 8:30 AM. The main hall of the Supreme Court is lined with busts of former chief justices; the courtroom itself is decorated with allegorical friezes. Perhaps the most interesting appurtenance in the imposing building, however, is a basketball court on one of the upper floors (it's been called the highest court in the land). *1st and E. Capitol Sts. NE, tel. 202/479–3000. Open weekdays 9–4:30.*

One block north of the Supreme Court, at the corner of Constitution Avenue and 2nd Street, is the redbrick **Sewall-Belmont House,** built in 1800 by Robert Sewall. Part of the house dates to 1680, making it the oldest home on Capitol Hill. From 1801 to 1813 Secretary of the Treasury Albert Gallatin lived here. He finalized the details of the Louisiana Purchase in his front-parlor office. The house became the only private residence burned in Washington during the British invasion of 1814, after a resident fired on advancing British troops from an upper-story window. The house is now the headquarters of the National Woman's Party and features a museum that chronicles the early days of the women's movement. The museum is filled with period furniture, and portraits and busts of suffrage movement leaders such as Lucretia Mott, Elizabeth Cady Stanton, and Alice Paul. *144*

Constitution Ave. NE, tel. 202/546–3989. Open Tues.–Fri. 10–3, weekends and most holidays noon–4.

After seeing the Sewall-Belmont House, continue east on Maryland Avenue, past the headquarters of the **Veterans of Foreign Wars.** Only three blocks from the Capitol, the Hill's residential character asserts itself. At Stanton Square turn right onto 4th Street NE, walk south two blocks, and then turn right onto A Street. The gray house with the mansard roof at 316 A **13** Street is the **Frederick Douglass Townhouse** (not open to the public). The first Washington home of the famous abolitionist and writer, this structure housed the Museum of African Art until 1987, when the museum was moved to a new building on the Mall.

Walk back to 4th Street and down another block to East Capitol Street, the border between the northeastern and southeastern quadrants of the city. The orange and yellow trash cans, emblazoned with the silhouette of an Indian, are reminders that East Capitol street is a main thoroughfare to RFK Stadium, home turf for the Washington Redskins. In the '50s there was a plan to construct government office buildings on both sides of East Capitol Street as far as Lincoln Park, seven blocks to the east. The neighborhood's active historic-preservation supporters successfully fought the proposal. **14** The houses on the **south side of East Capitol Street** are a representative sampling of homes on the Hill. The corner house, No. 329, has a striking tower with a bay window and stained-glass. Next door are two Victorian houses with iron trim below the second floor. A pre–Civil War, Greek-Revival frame house sits behind a trim garden at No. 317. The alley to the right of No. 317 also dates from the 19th century. The two parallel rows of bricks were intended for carriage wheels, while the stones in the center **15** were trod by horses' hooves. At **326 A St.,** in a quiet neighborhood behind the Library of Congress's Adams Building, is the stucco house that artist Constantino Brumidi lived in while he was working on the Capitol.

Time Out **Duddington's** (319 Pennsylvania Ave. SE), named for a large estate laid out on this site in the 17th century, serves up burgers, subs, and pizza made with fresh dough. The sushi-serving **Suehiro** (332 Pennsylvania Ave. SE) is a little more exotic. For dessert, sample the pastries and cookies at **Sherrill's Bakery** (233 Pennsylvania Ave. SE).

Turn right on Pennsylvania Avenue and head back toward the Capitol's familiar white dome. The south side of the street is lined with restaurants and bars frequented by those who live and work on the Hill.

You'll find the nearest Metro stop, Capitol South, on the corner of 1st and D streets SE.

Tour 5: Georgetown

Numbers in the margin correspond to points of interest on the Tour 5: Georgetown map.

Long before the District of Columbia was formed, Georgetown, Washington's oldest neighborhood, was a separate city that boasted a harbor full of ships and warehouses filled with tobacco. Washington has filled in around Georgetown over the years, but the former tobacco port retains an air of aloofness. Its narrow streets, which refuse to conform to Pierre L'Enfant's plan for the Federal City, make up the capital's wealthiest neighborhood and are the nucleus of its nightlife.

This is Washington's center for restaurants, bars, nightclubs, and trendy boutiques. On M Street and Wisconsin Avenue, visitors can indulge just about any taste and take home almost any up-market souvenir. Harder to find is a parking place. The lack of a Metro station in Georgetown means you'll have to take a bus or walk to this part of Washington. It is a leisurely stroll from either the Foggy Bottom or Dupont Circle Metro stops.

❶ Start your exploration of Georgetown in front of the **Old Stone House** (M Street between 30th and 31st streets), thought to be Washington's only surviving pre-Revolutionary building. Built in 1764 by a cabinetmaker named Christopher

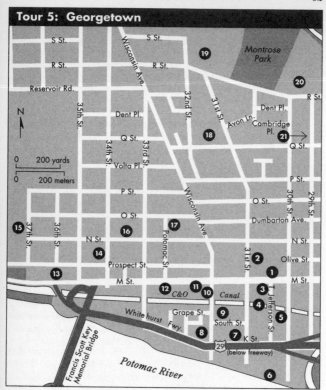

Tour 5: Georgetown

Chesapeake &
Ohio Canal, **4**

Cox's Row, **16**

Customs
House, **2**

Dodge
Warehouse, **8**

Dumbarton
House, **21**

Dumbarton
Oaks, **19**

Exorcist
steps, **13**

Foundry Mall, **5**

Georgetown
Park, **11**

Georgetown
University, **15**

Grace Episcopal
Church, **9**

Halcyon
House, **14**

Market-
house,**12**

Masonic lodge, **3**

Oak Hill
Cemetery, **20**

Old Stone
House, **1**

St. John's
Church, **17**

Suter's Tavern, **7**

Tudor Place, **18**

Vigilant
Firehouse, **10**

Washington
Harbour, **6**

Layman, this fieldstone house was used both as a residence and a place of business by a succession of occupants. Five of the house's rooms are furnished with the sort of sturdy beds, spinning wheels, and simple tables associated with middle-class Colonial America. The National Park Service maintains the house and its lovely gardens in the rear, which are planted with fruit trees and seasonal blooms. Costumed guides answer questions about the house and its history. *3051 M St. NW, tel. 202/426-6851. Open Wed.–Sun. 8–4:30.*

Around the corner, at 1221 31st Street, is the old Renaissance Revival–style **Customs House.** Built in 1858 to serve the port of Georgetown, it's been transformed into the Georgetown branch of the U.S. Postal Service, and there's really no reason to go inside unless you want to buy stamps or mail postcards.

Go back to M Street and cross over to Thomas Jefferson Street (between 30th and 31st streets). For most of its history, Georgetown was a working city, and the original names of its streets—Water Street, The Keys, Fishing Lane—bear witness to the importance of the harbor. The area south of M Street (originally called Bridge Street because of the bridge that spanned Rock Creek to the east) was inhabited by tradesmen, laborers, and merchants. Their homes were modest and close to Georgetown's industrial heart. The two-story brick building at 1083 **Thomas Jefferson Street** was built around 1865 as a stable for the horses and hearses of a nearby undertaker and cabinetmaker. The wide doors on the right let the horses in, while the hoist beam above the right-most window was used to lift hay and wood to the second floor. Three fine brick Federal houses stand south of the Georgetown Dutch Inn, at 1069, 1067, and 1063 Thomas Jefferson Street. The last has attractive flat lintels with keystones and a rounded keystone arch above the doorway. Across the street, at No. 1058, is a two-story brick structure built around 1810 as a **Masonic lodge.** It features interesting detailing, including a pointed facade and recessed central arch, proof of the Masons' traditional attachment to the building arts.

(4) As you walk south on Thomas Jefferson Street, you'll pass over the **Chesapeake & Ohio Canal,** the waterway that kept Georgetown open to shipping after its harbor had filled with silt. George Washington was one of the first to advance the idea of a canal linking the Potomac with the Ohio River across the Appalachians. Work started on the C & O Canal in 1828, and when it opened in 1850, its 74 locks linked Georgetown with Cumberland, Maryland, 184 miles to the northwest (still short of its intended destination). Lumber, coal, iron, wheat, and flour moved up and down the canal, but it was never as successful as its planners had hoped it would be. Many of the bridges spanning the canal in Georgetown were too low to allow anything other than fully loaded barges to pass underneath, and competition from the Baltimore & Ohio Railroad eventually spelled an end to profitability. Today the canal is a part of the National Park system, and walkers follow the towpath once used by mules while canoers paddle the canal's calm waters. Between April and October you can go on a leisurely, mule-drawn trip aboard *The Georgetown* canal barge. Tick-**(5)** ets are available across the canal, in the **Foundry Mall** (1055 Thomas Jefferson St., NW, tel. 202/ 472–4376).

(6) Continue south, across K Street, and into **Washington Harbour,** a glittering, postmodern riverfront development designed by Arthur Cotton Moore that includes restaurants, offices, and apartments, and upscale shops. The plazas around its large central fountain and gardens are dotted with the eerily realistic sculptures of J. Seward Johnson, Jr. From the edge of Washington Harbour you can see the Watergate complex and Kennedy Center to the east.

Time Out If the breeze off the river has given you an appetite, stop at **Artie's Harbour Deli Cafe** for a sandwich. For dessert, select from the **Café Rosé's** waistline-threatening selection of authentic Viennese pastries. Both are in the Washington Harbour complex.

Georgetown's **K Street** is lined with the offices of architects, ad agencies, and public relations companies. In many of these offices you can hear the rumble of cars on the Whitehurst Freeway, the elevated road above K Street that leads to the Francis Scott Key Memorial Bridge. Though you'll probably have to peer through a vine-covered fence to see it, at the corner of 31st and K streets is a plaque commemorating **Suter's Tavern.** In March 1791, in the one-story hostelry that once stood on this spot, George Washington met with the men who owned the tobacco farms and swampy marshes to the east of Georgetown and convinced them to sell their land to the government so that construction could begin on the District of Columbia.

At the foot of Wisconsin Avenue is another legacy from the area's mercantile past. The last three buildings on the west side were built around 1830 by trader and merchant **Francis Dodge.** Note the heavy stone foundation of the southernmost **warehouse,** its star-end braces and the broken hoist in the gable end. According to an 1838 newspaper ad, Georgetown shoppers could visit Dodge's grocery to buy such items as "Porto Rico Sugar, Marseilles soft-shelled Almonds and Havanna Segars."

Halfway up Wisconsin Avenue, on the other side of the street, stands the Gothic Revival **Grace Episcopal Church.** In the mid-to-late-19th century this church served the boatmen and workers from the nearby C & O Canal. At the time this was one of the poorest sections of Georgetown. (There are no "poor" sections in Georgetown anymore.)

Walking farther up Wisconsin Avenue you'll again cross the C & O Canal, this time via the only bridge that remains from the 19th century. On the north side is a simple granite obelisk honoring the men who built the waterway. A memorial of a more poignant sort can be found at the 1840 **Vigilant Firehouse,** north of the canal at 1066 Wisconsin Avenue. A plaque set in the wall reads: "Bush, the Old Fire Dog, died of Poison, July 5th, 1869, R.I.P."

The intersection of Wisconsin Avenue and M Street is the heart of boisterous Georgetown.

This spot—under the gleaming, golden dome of Riggs Bank on the northeast corner—is mobbed every weekend.

⑪ Turning left on M Street you'll come to the entrance to **Georgetown Park** (3222 M St. NW), a multilevel shopping extravaganza that answers the question "If the Victorians had invented shopping malls, what would they look like?" Such high-ticket stores as FAO Schwarz, Liberty of London, Polo/Ralph Lauren, and Godiva Chocolates can be found within this artful, skylit mass of polished brass, tile flooring, and potted plants. If you've always looked down your nose at mall architecture, Georgetown Park might win you over.

Time Out   **Pizzeria Uno** (3211 M St.) has brought Chicago-style pizza to the heart of Georgetown. The deep-dish pies take a while to cook, but the wait is worth it. Those in a hurry may want to order the "personal-sized" pizza with soup or a salad: It's ready in five minutes and costs less than $5. Further up is **Madurai** (3318 M St. NW), a smallish, second-floor restaurant specializing in spicy vegetarian Indian cuisine.

A stroll up either M Street or Wisconsin Avenue will take you past a dizzying array of merchandise, from expensive bicycling accessories to ropes of gold, from antique jewelry and furniture to the latest fashions in clothes and records. Walking west on M Street you'll come to the 1865 **⑫** **Markethouse,** a brick market stall across from Potomac Street. There's been a market on this site since 1795, but the restored Markethouse sits empty, waiting for the right developer to breathe life into it.

M Street to the west leads to the **Key Bridge** into Rosslyn, Virginia. A house owned by Francis Scott Key, author of the national anthem, was demolished in 1947 to make way for the bridge that would bear his name. A nonprofit organization has been formed to build a memorial park on the small triangle of clear ground near the bridge.

The heights of Georgetown to the north above N Street contrast with the busy jumble of the old waterfront. To reach the higher ground you can walk up M Street past the old brick streetcar barn at No. 3600 (now a block of offices), turn right, and climb the 75 steps that figured prominently in the eerie climax of the movie *The Exorcist.* If you would prefer a less demanding climb, walk up 34th Street instead.

⑭ Halcyon House, at the corner of 34th and Prospect streets, was built in 1783 by Benjamin Stoddert, first secretary of the Navy. The object of many subsequent additions and renovations, the house is now a concatenation of architectural styles. Prospect Street gets its name from the fine views it affords of the waterfront and the river below.

The sounds of traffic diminish the farther north one walks from the bustle of M Street. To the ⑮ west is **Georgetown University,** the oldest Jesuit school in the country. It was founded in 1789 by John Carroll, first American bishop and first archbishop of Baltimore. About 12,000 students attend Georgetown, known now as much for its perennially successful basketball team as for its fine programs in law, medicine, and the liberal arts. When seen from the Potomac or from Washington's high ground, the Gothic spires of Georgetown's older buildings give the university an almost medieval look.

Architecture buffs, especially those interested in Federal and Victorian houses, enjoy wandering along the redbrick sidewalks of upper Georgetown. Many of the homes here are larger and more luxurious than their waterfront counterparts, having been built by the harbor's wealthier citizens. Georgetown is today the home of Washington's elite, and the average house in upper Georgetown has two signs on it: a brass plaque notifying passersby of the building's historic interest and a window decal that warns burglars of its state-of-the-art alarm system. To get a representative taste of the houses in the area, continue north for a block on 34th Street and turn right onto N Street. The group of five Federal houses between 3339 and 3327 N ⑯ Street are known collectively as **Cox's Row,** after John Cox, a former mayor of Georgetown, who built them in 1817.

The flat-fronted, redbrick Federal house at **3307 N Street** was the home of then-Senator John F. Kennedy and his family before the White House beckoned. Turn left onto Potomac and walk a block up to O Street. O Street still has two left-overs from an earlier age: cobblestones and streetcar tracks. Residents are proud of the cobblestones, and you'll notice that even some of the concrete patches have been scored to resemble the paving stones. **St. John's Church** (3240 O St. NW, tel. 202/338–1796) was built in 1809 and is attributed to Dr. William Thornton, architect of the Capitol. Later alterations have left it looking more Victorian than Federal. At the corner of the churchyard is a memorial to Colonel Ninian Beall, the Scotsman who received the original patent for the land that would become Georgetown.

Make your way to Q Street between 31st and 32nd streets. Through the trees to the north, at the top of a sloping lawn, you'll see the neoclassical **Tudor Place,** designed by Capitol architect William Thornton and completed in 1816. The house was built for Thomas Peter, son of Georgetown's first mayor, and his wife Martha Custis, Martha Washington's granddaughter. It was because of this connection to the president's family that Tudor Place came to house many items from Mount Vernon. The yellow stucco house is interesting for its architecture—especially the dramatic, two-story domed portico on the south side—but its familial heritage is even more remarkable: Tudor Place stayed in the same family for 178 years, until 1983, when Armistead Peter III died. Before his death, Peter established a foundation to restore the house and open it to the public. On a house tour you'll see chairs that belonged to George Washington, Francis Scott Key's desk, and spurs of members of the Peter family who were killed in the Civil War (although the house was in Washington, the family was true to its Virginia roots and fought for Dixie). The grounds contain many specimens planted in the early 19th century. *1644 31st St. NW, tel. 202/ 965–0400. Tours Tues.–Sat. 10, 11:30, 1, and 2:30. Admission: $5. Reservations required.*

⑲ Dumbarton Oaks—not to be confused with the nearby Dumbarton House—is on 32nd Street, north of R Street. Career diplomat Robert Woods Bliss and his wife, Mildred, heiress to the Fletcher's Castoria fortune, bought the property in 1920 and set about taming the sprawling grounds and removing 19th-century additions that had marred the Federal lines of the 1801 mansion. In 1940 the Blisses conveyed the estate to Harvard University, which maintains world-renowned collections of Byzantine and pre-Columbian art there. The Byzantine museum includes secular and religious items, with beautiful examples of metalwork, enameling, ivory carving, and manuscript illumination. Pre-Columbian works—artifacts and textiles from Mexico and Central and South America—are arranged in an enclosed glass pavilion designed by Philip Johnson.

Anyone with even a mild interest in flowers, shrubs, trees—anything that grows out of the ground—will enjoy a visit to Dumbarton Oaks' 10 acres of formal gardens, one of the loveliest spots in all of Washington (enter via R Street). Designed by noted landscape architect Beatrix Farrand, the gardens incorporate elements of traditional English, Italian, and French styles. A full-time crew of a dozen gardeners toils to maintain the stunning collection of terraces, geometric gardens, tree-shaded brick walks, fountains, arbors, and pools. Plenty of well-positioned benches make this a good place for resting weary feet, too. *Art collections: 1703 32nd St. NW, tel. 202/338–8278 (recorded information) or 202/342–3200. Open Tues.–Sun. 2–5. Suggested donation for art collections: $1. Gardens: 31st and R Sts. NW. Open Apr. 1–Oct. 31, daily 2–6. Admission: $2 adults, $1 senior citizens and children, senior citizens free on Wed.; Nov. 1–Mar. 31, daily 2–5. Admission: free. Both gardens and collections are closed on national holidays and Christmas eve.*

Three other sylvan retreats lie north of R Street in upper Georgetown. Originally part of the Bliss estate, **Dumbarton Oaks Park** sprawls to the north and west. **Montrose Park** lies to the **⑳** east of the estate. Further east is **Oak Hill Cemetery,** its funerary obelisks, crosses, and gravestones spread out like an amphitheater of the dead on a hill overlooking Rock Creek. Near the entrance is an 1850 Gothic-style chapel designed by Smithsonian Castle architect James Renwick. Across from the chapel is the resting place of actor, playwright, and diplomat John H. Payne, who is remembered today primarily for his song "Home Sweet Home." A few hundred feet to the north is the circular tomb of William Corcoran, founder of the Corcoran Gallery of Art. *30th and R Sts. NW, tel. 202/337–2835. Open weekdays 9–4:30.*

㉑ A few steps east of 28th Street on Q Street is **Dumbarton House,** the headquarters of the National Society of the Colonial Dames of America. Its symmetry and the two distinctive bow wings on the north side make Dumbarton a distinctive example of Federal architecture. The man who built the house, Joseph Nourse, was registrar of the U.S. Treasury. Other well-known Americans have spent time at the house, including Dolley Madison, who is said to have stopped here when fleeing Washington in 1814. One hundred years later, the house was moved 50 feet up the hill, when Q Street was cut through to the Dumbarton Bridge.

Eight rooms inside Dumbarton House have been restored to their Colonial splendor and are decorated with period furnishings such as mahogany American Chippendale chairs, hallmark silver, Persian rugs, and a breakfront cabinet filled with rare books. Notable items include a 1789 Charles Willson Peale portrait of Benjamin Stoddert's children (with an early view of Georgetown harbor in the background), Martha Washington's traveling cloak, and a British redcoat's red coat. The house is currently closed for renovation that's expected to be finished in the spring of 1993. *2715 Q St. NW, tel. 703/556–0881.*

Tour 6: Alexandria

Numbers in the margin correspond to points of interest on the Tour 6: Alexandria map.

Just a short Metro ride (or bike ride) away from Washington, Old Town Alexandria today attracts visitors seeking a break from the monuments and hustle-and-bustle of the District and interested in an encounter with America's Colonial heritage. Founded in 1749 by Scottish merchants eager to capitalize on the booming tobacco trade, Alexandria emerged as one of the most important ports in Colonial America. The city's history is linked to the most significant events and personages of the Colonial and Revolutionary periods. This colorful past is still alive in restored 18th- and 19th-century homes, churches, and taverns; in the cobbled streets; and on the revitalized waterfront, where clipper ships dock and artisans display their wares.

The quickest way to get to Old Town is to take the Metro to the King Street stop (about 25 minutes from Metro Center). If you're driving you can take either the George Washington Memorial Parkway or Jefferson Davis Highway (Route 1) south from Arlington.

❶ The best place to start a tour of Old Town is at the **Alexandria Convention & Visitors Bureau,** which is in **Ramsay House,** the home of the town's first postmaster and lord mayor, William Ramsay. The structure is believed to be the oldest house in Alexandria. Ramsay was a Scotsman, as a swath of his tartan on the door proclaims. Travel counselors here provide information, brochures, and self-guided walking tours of the town. *221 King St. 22314, tel. 703/ 838–4200. Open daily 9–5. Closed Thanksgiving, Christmas, and New Year's Day. Out-of-towners are given a 72-hr courtesy parking permit that allows them to park free at any 2-hr metered spot.*

❷ Across the street, at the corner of Fairfax and King streets, is the **Stabler-Leadbeater Apothecary Shop,** the second-oldest apothecary in the country. It was patronized by George Washington and the Lee family, and it was here, on October 17, 1859, that Lt. Col. Robert E. Lee received orders to move to Harper's Ferry to suppress John Brown's insurrection. The shop now houses a small museum of 18th-century apothecary memorabilia, including one of the finest collections of apothecary bottles in the country (some 800 bottles in all). *105–107 S.*

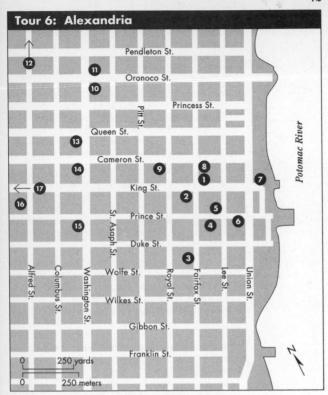

Tour 6: Alexandria

Alexandria Black History Resource Center, **12**

Alexandria Convention & Visitors Bureau, **1**

Athenaeum, **5**

Boyhood home of Robert E. Lee, **11**

Captain's Row, **6**

Carlyle House, **8**

Christ Church, **14**

Friendship Fire Company, **16**

Gadsby's Tavern Museum, **9**

George Washington Masonic National Memorial, **17**

Lee-Fendall House, **10**

Lloyd House, **13**

Lyceum, **15**

Old Presbyterian Meeting House, **3**

Stabler-Leadbeater Apothecary Shop, **2**

Torpedo Factory Arts Center, **7**

*Fairfax St., tel. 703/836–3713. Open Mon.–
Tues. and Thurs.–Sat. 10–4, Sun. noon–4.*

Two blocks south on Fairfax Street, just beyond
Duke Street, stands the **Old Presbyterian Meeting House** (321 S. Fairfax St., tel. 703/549–
6670). Built in 1774, this was an important meeting place for Scottish patriots during the Revolution. Eulogies for George Washington were
delivered here on December 29, 1799. In a corner of the churchyard you'll find the **Tomb of the
Unknown Soldier of the American Revolution.**

Next walk back up Fairfax Street one block and
turn right on Prince Street. The block between
Fairfax and Lee streets is known as **Gentry
Row.** One of the most noteworthy structures in
the city is the **Athenaeum,** at the corner of
Prince and Lee streets. The striking, reddish-
brown Greek Revival edifice was built as a bank
in the 1850s.

The next block of Prince Street to the east (between Lee and Union streets) is known as
Captain's Row because this was where many of
the city's sea captains built their homes. The
cobblestones in the street were allegedly laid by
Hessian mercenaries who fought for the British
during the Revolutionary War and who were being held in Alexandria as prisoners of war.

Continuing east on Prince Street you'll come to
Alexandria's lively waterfront. Two blocks to
the north up Union Street (at the foot of King
Street) is one of the most popular destinations in
the city, the **Torpedo Factory Arts Center.** This
former munitions plant (yes, naval torpedoes
were actually manufactured here during World
War I and World War II) has now been converted
into studios and galleries for some 175 professional artists. Almost every imaginable medium
is represented, from printmaking and sculpture
to jewelry making, pottery, and stained glass.
Visitors can view the artisans' workshops, and
most of the artworks are for sale at reasonable
prices. *105 N. Union St., tel. 703/838–4565.
Open daily 10–5.*

Moving back into the town, a two-block walk up
Cameron Street brings you to the grandest of
the older houses in the town, **Carlyle House,** at

the corner of North Fairfax Street. Patterned after a Scottish country manor house, the structure was completed in 1753 by Scottish merchant John Carlyle. This was General Braddock's headquarters and the place where he met with five Royal Governors in 1755 to plan the strategy and funding of the early campaigns of the French and Indian War. *121 N. Fairfax St., tel. 703/549–2997. Open Tues.–Sat. 10–5, Sun. noon–5.*

⑨ One block west on Royal Street is **Gadsby's Tavern Museum,** housed in the old City Tavern and Hotel, which was a center of political and social life in the late 18th century. George Washington attended birthday celebrations in the ballroom here. A tour of the facilities takes you through the taproom, game room, assembly room, ballroom, and communal bedrooms. *134–138 N. Royal St., tel. 703/838–4242. Open Tues.–Sat. 10–5, Sun. 1–5.*

Continue west on Cameron Street for three blocks and turn right on Washington Street. The corner of Washington and Oronoco streets (three blocks north) is known as **Lee Corner** because at one time a Lee-owned house stood on each of the four corners. Two survive. One is the

⑩ **Lee-Fendall House,** the home of several illustrious members of the Lee family, including Richard Henry Lee, signer of the Declaration of Independence, and cavalry commander "Light Horse Harry" Lee. *614 Oronoco St., tel. 703/548–1789. Open Tues.–Sat. 10–4, Sun. noon–4.*

⑪ Directly across the street is the **boyhood home of Robert E. Lee,** a fine example of a 19th-century town house. It features Federal architecture and antique furnishings and paintings. *607 Oronoco St., tel. 703/548–8454. Open Mon.–Sat. 10–4, Sun. 1–4. Closed Dec. 15–Feb. 1 except on Sunday closest to Jan. 19 for Lee's birthday celebration. Occasionally closed for weekend weddings.*

Alexandria's history isn't all Washingtons and Lees, however. The Federal census of 1790 recorded 52 free blacks living in the city and the port town was one of the largest slave exportation points in the South, with at least two bustling slave markets. The history of African

Americans in Alexandria and Virginia from 1749 to the present is recounted at the **⑫ Alexandria Black History Resource Center,** two blocks north and two blocks west of Lee's boyhood home. *638 North Alfred St., tel. 703/838–4356. Open Tues.–Sat. 10–4.*

Head back to Washington Street and move south now all the way to the corner of Queen Street. **⑬** Here you'll find the **Lloyd House,** a fine example of Georgian architecture. Built in 1797, it is now operated as part of the Alexandria Library and houses a collection of rare books and documents relating to city and state history. *220 North Washington St., tel. 703/838–4577. Open Mon.–Sat. 9–5.*

At the corner of Cameron and Washington **⑭** streets, one block south, stands **Christ Church** (118 N. Washington St., tel. 703/549–1450. Open Mon.–Sat. 9–4, Sun. 1–4), where both Washington and Lee were pewholders (Washington paid 36 pounds and 10 shillings, a lot of money in those days, for Pew 60). Built in 1773, it is a fine example of an English, Georgian country-style church. The interior features a fine Palladian window, interior balcony, and a wrought-brass-and-crystal chandelier brought from England at Washington's expense.

From Christ Church, walk two blocks south to **⑮** the **Lyceum** at the corner of Washington and Prince streets. Built in 1839, the structure served alternately as the Alexandria Library, a Civil War hospital, a residence, and an office building. It was restored in the '70s and now houses two art galleries, a gift shop, and a museum devoted to the area's history. A limited amount of travel information for the entire state is also available here. *201 S. Washington St., tel. 703/838–4994. Open daily 10–5. Closed Thanksgiving, Christmas, and New Year's Day.*

Two blocks to the west on South Alfred Street is **⑯** the **Friendship Fire Company.** George Washington was a founder of the volunteer company and was its honorary captain. On display is a replica of the $400 fire engine that Washington bought, considered at the time to be the finest obtainable. *107 S. Alfred St. Irregular operating hours.*

⑰ A little far to walk but well worth visiting is the **George Washington Masonic National Memorial** on Callahan Drive at King Street, a mile west of the center of the city. The memorial's spire dominates the surroundings, and from the entryway visitors get a spectacular view of Alexandria and Washington in the distance. Among other things, the building contains furnishings from the first Masonic lodge in Alexandria, in which George Washington was Worshipful Master at the same time he served as president. *101 Callahan Dr., tel. 703/683-2007. Open daily 9-5. Closed Thanksgiving, Christmas, and New Year's Day. Free guided tours of the building and observation deck daily 9:15-4:10.*

Washington for Free

Visitors will have a hard time finding attractions and events in Washington that are *not* free. There are no admission fees to any of the Smithsonian museums—including the National Zoo—and entry to many other museums and galleries is also without charge. The ride to the top of the Washington Monument used to cost a dime, but today, like admission to the rest of the memorials, that's free, too.

Concerts **Fort Dupont Summer Theater** (Minnesota Ave. and F St. SE, tel. 202/426-7723) hosts well-known jazz artists Friday and Saturday evenings at 8:30 during the summer.

The National Building Museum's impressive Pension Building (F St. between 4th and 5th Sts. NW, tel. 202/272-2448) is the site of lunchtime concerts the fourth Wednesday of each month.

The National Symphony Orchestra (tel. 202/416-8100) presents free concerts on the West Lawn of the Capitol on Memorial Day and Labor Day weekends and on July 4th. The orchestra also offers free classical concerts at the National Gallery of Art (6th St. and Constitution Ave. NW, tel. 202/842-6941) Sunday evenings from October to June.

The National Theatre (1321 Pennsylvania Ave. NW, tel. 202/783-3372) hosts a wide-ranging free performance series of music, dance, readings, and one-act plays each Monday night from February to May and October to December.

"Monday Night at the National" performances are held at 7 PM and 8:30 PM.

The Sylvan Theater (tel. 202/619–7222), on the grounds of the Washington Monument, is the site of numerous military and big-band concerts from mid-June to August.

Lectures   **The Library of Congress** (tel. 202/707–5394 or 202/707–2905) sponsors periodic literary lectures and poetry readings by well-known poets, usually on Thursday evenings.

The Martin Luther King Memorial Library's "Lunchtime Author Series" (901 G St. NW, tel. 202/727–1186) features readings and discussions with local and national authors every Tuesday at noon, except during the month of June.

The Smithsonian Institution (tel. 202/357–2700) offers free lectures, demonstrations, and gallery talks by both visiting scholars and Smithsonian fellows at many of its museums on and off the Mall.

The "Weekend" section in Friday's *Washington Post* is an excellent source of other free events in and around the District.

What to See and Do with Children

Kids who have been learning about the early days of America or how its government works will find much to see and enjoy in Washington. History that seems dusty and boring in a textbook comes alive at the White House, the Senate Chamber, and the Supreme Court. For younger children (or less politically-minded tykes) numerous museums encourage hands-on learning. For other kid-oriented fare, consult the "Carousel" listings in the Friday *Washington Post* "Weekend" section.

Academy of Model Aviation. The 150,000-member academy helps regulate model aviation activities thoughout the country. Here, in the atrium of the group's headquarters, you'll find dozens of planes on display, everything from a tiny flyable craft with a 6½-inch wingspan to a six-foot-long model of an F-104 Starfighter. Engines, radio control equipment, and club patches are also exhibited. A computer flight simulator game allows would-be pilots to test their skills. *1810 Samuel Morse Dr., Reston, Va., tel. 703/435–0750. Open weekdays 9–5, Sat. 10–3.*

Adventure Theater (MacArthur Blvd. and Goldsboro Rd., Glen Echo, MD, tel. 301/320–5331). Delightful plays for children ages four and up are performed year-round at the Glen Echo Park. Performances are Saturday and Sunday at 1:30 and 3:30. Reservations suggested.

Capital Children's Museum In this hands-on museum children can send messages in Morse code, hoist cinder blocks with pulleys and levers, crawl through a mock sewer, climb on a fire engine, and learn about foreign countries by making traditional ethnic foods and crafts. *800 3rd St. NE, tel. 202/543–8600. Open daily 10–5. Closed Thanksgiving, Christmas, New Year's Day, and Easter. Admission: $5 for ages 2–59, senior citizens $2, children under 2 free.*

D.A.R Museum (*see* Tour 3: The White House, above). Free "Colonial Adventure" tours are held the first and third Sundays of the month. Costumed docents lead children aged five through seven through the museum, explaining the exhibits and describing life in Colonial America. Make reservations at least 10 days in advance by calling 202/879–3239. *Metro stop, Farragut West.*

Discovery Theater (900 Jefferson Dr. SW, tel. 202/357–1500). Plays, puppet shows, and storytellers are featured at this theater October through June, in the west hall of the Smithsonian's Arts and Industries Building. *Metro stop, Smithsonian.*

National Air and Space Museum, National Museum of American History, National Museum of Natural History (*see* Tour 1: The Mall, above). *Metro stop, Smithsonian or Federal Triangle.*

National Geographic Explorer's Hall (*see* Other Attractions, below). *Metro stop, Farragut North.*

The National Zoo (*see* Other Attractions, below). *Metro stop, Cleveland Park or Woodley Park/National Zoo.*

"Saturday Morning at the National" (1321 Pennsylvania Ave. NW, tel. 202/783–3372). This performance series for youngsters has featured such acts as mimes, puppet shows, dance troupes, magicians, and children's theater groups. The performances are free, on a first-come, first-seated basis, at the National Theater, Saturdays at 9:30 AM and 11 AM. *Metro stop, Metro Center.*

Tidal Basin paddle boats (*see* Tour 2: The Monuments, above). *Metro stop, Smithsonian.*

Washington Dolls' House and Toy Museum. Founded in 1975 by a dollhouse historian, this compact museum contains a charming collection of American and imported dolls, dollhouses, toys, and games, most from the Victorian period. Highlights of the collection include a miniature Teddy Roosevelt on safari and an 1884 model of the Capitol. Miniature accessories, dollhouse kits, and antique toys and games are on sale in the museum's shops. *5236 44th St. NW, tel. 202/244–0024. Admission: $3 adults, $2 senior citizens, $1 children under 14. Open Tues.–Sat. 10–5, Sun. noon–5. Metro stop, Friendship Heights.*

The Washington Monument (*see* Tour 2: The Monuments, above). *Metro stops, Federal Triangle or Smithsonian.*

Other Attractions

Arlington National Cemetery, across the river in Virginia, is the final resting place of some 200,000 souls, including Robert and John F. Kennedy, some of the shuttle Challenger astronauts, sailors killed in the explosion of the USS *Maine,* and the Unknown Soldiers, above whose tomb a precision unit stands guard. There is a wonderful view of Washington from the front of Arlington House—a Greek Revival house on the grounds of the cemetery that was once owned by Robert E. Lee. *West end of Memorial Bridge, Arlington, VA, tel. 703/692–0931. Open Apr.–Sept. daily 8–7; Oct.–Mar. daily 8–5. Metro stop, Arlington Cemetery.*

The **National Geographic Society's Explorer's Hall** is like the magazine come to life. Visitors are invited to learn about the world in decidedly interactive ways. The most dramatic events take place in Earth Station One, a 72-seat amphitheater that literally sends the audience on a journey around the world, "the world" in this case being a huge, hand-painted globe that floats and spins on a cushion of air. *17th and M Sts. NW, tel. 202/857-7588. Open Mon.–Sat. and holidays 9–5, Sun. 10–5. Admission free. Metro stop, Farragut North.*

Ford's Theatre looks much as it did on April 14, 1865, the night Abraham Lincoln was shot while watching a performance of *Our American Cousin.* While that play is no longer in the repertoire, Ford's is still used as a theater, home mainly to shows with family appeal. The basement houses a museum with such artifacts as Booth's pistol and the clothes Lincoln was wearing when he was assassinated. Across the street is the Petersen House, where the president was carried after he was wounded and where he died the next day. *511 10th St. NW, tel. 202/426-6924. Open daily 9–5. Theater closed when rehearsals or matinees are in progress (generally Thurs. and weekends). Lincoln Museum in basement remains open at these times. Closed Christmas. Admission free. Metro stop, Metro Center.*

Frederick Douglass National Historic Site. Cedar Hill, the Anacostia home of noted abolitionist Frederick Douglass, was the first place designated by Congress as a Black National Historic site. Douglass, an ex-slave who delivered fiery antislavery speeches at home and abroad, was 60 when he moved here in 1877. The house has a wonderful view of the Federal City, across the Anacostia River, and contains many of Douglass's personal belongings. *1411 W St. SE, tel. 202/426-5961. Open fall and winter, daily 9–4; spring and summer daily 9–5. Tours given on the hour. Admission free. Metro stop, Anacostia.*

Mount Vernon—south of the capital, in Virginia—had been in the Washington family for nearly 90 years by the time George inherited it all in 1761. The main house, with its red roof, is elegant though understated. The inside of the building is more ornate, especially the formal receiving room with its molded ceiling decorated with agricultural motifs. Throughout the house you'll find other, smaller symbols of the owner's eminence, such as a key to the main portal of the Bastille, presented to Washington by the Marquis de Lafayette; Washington's Presidential chair; and a case of traveling wine bottles. Small groups of visitors are ushered from room to room, each of which is staffed by a guide who describes the furnishings and answers questions. Don't miss the view of the Potomac River from the back of the house. *Tel. 703/ 780–2000. Open Mar.–Oct. 9–5, Nov.–Feb. 9–4. Admission: $6 adults, $5.50 senior citizens 62 and older, $3 children 6–11 accompanied by adults.*

The **National Archives** is where you'll find the Declaration of Independence, the Constitution, and the Bill of Rights. The famous documents are in the Rotunda, inside a helium-filled case made of bulletproof glass that's lowered into a vault every evening. *Constitution Ave. between 7th and 9th Sts. NW, tel. 202/501–5000. Open Apr.–Labor Day, daily 10–9; Sept.–Mar. daily 10–5:30. Admission free. Metro stop, Archives.*

The **National Museum of American Art** and the **National Portrait Gallery** share the Greek Revival–style Old Patent Office Building in what's known as Washington's old downtown. The National Museum of American Art's collection comprises works from the country's infancy, large-scale landscapes by Albert Bierstadt and Thomas Moran, paintings by American Impressionists like John Henry Twachtman and Childe Hassam, and modern works by Jasper Johns and Robert Rauschenberg.

Exhibits in the National Portrait Gallery include the Hall of Presidents (featuring a portrait or sculpture of each chief executive), the George Washington "Lansdowne" portrait, and paintings and photographs of athletes, entertainers and the otherwise famous. The Victorian Renaissance third floor features a Civil War display, with portraits, photographs, and lithographs of such wartime personalities as Julia Ward Howe, Ulysses S. Grant, and Robert E.

Lee. *8th and F Sts. NW, tel. 202/357–2700.
Open daily 10–5:30. Closed Christmas. Admission free. Metro stop, Gallery Place.*

The **National Zoological Park,** part of the Smithsonian Institution, is one of the foremost zoos in the world. Innovative compounds show many animals in naturalistic settings, including the Great Flight Cage, a walk-in aviary in which birds fly unrestricted. Giant crabs, octopuses, cuttlefish, and worms are displayed in an invertebrate exhibit. The 160-acre zoo has had success breeding vertebrates, too, including red pandas, golden lion tamarins, and pygmy hippopotamuses. Amazonia, an ambitious display recreating the complete ecosystem of a South American rainforest, is scheduled to open in the spring of 1992. *3001 Connecticut Ave. NW, tel. 202/673–4717. Open May 1–Sept. 1, daily: grounds 8–8, animal buildings 8–6; Sept. 16– Apr. 30, daily: grounds 8–6, animal buildings 9–6. Closed Christmas. Admission free. Metro stop, Woodley Park–Zoo.*

The **Pentagon** is an exercise in immensity: 23,000 military and civilian employees work in the Department of Defense headquarters; it is as wide as three Washington Monuments laid end to end; inside are 17½ miles of corridors, 7,754 windows, and 691 drinking fountains. The 45-minute tour of the five-sided building takes you past hallways lined with portraits of past and present military leaders, scale models of ships and planes, and into the Hall of Heroes, where the names of all the Congressional Medal of Honor winners are inscribed. *Off I–395, Arlington, VA, tel. 703/695–1776. Tours weekdays every half-hour 9:30–3:30. Closed on Federal holidays. Admission free. Metro stop, Pentagon.*

The 1,800 acres of **Rock Creek Park** have provided a cool oasis for Washingtonians since Congress set them aside in 1890. There's a lot to enjoy here, including picnic sites, biking and hiking trails, and groves of dogwoods, beeches, oaks, and cedar. Rangers at the Nature Center and Planetarium (south of Military Road at 5000 Glover Rd. NW, tel. 202/426–6829) will acquaint you with the park and advise you of scheduled activities. One of the highlights in Pierce Mill, a restored 19th-century gristmill powered by the water of Rock Creek (tel. 202/426–6908). *Between 16th St. and Connecticut Ave. NW, tel. 202/426–6829 for park activities. Park open daylight hours only.*

3 **Shopping**

Shopping Districts

*by Deborah
Papier*

Georgetown remains Washington's favorite
shopping area. Though it is not on a subway line,
and parking is impossible, people still flock
here. The attraction (aside from the lively street
scene) is the profusion of specialty shops, which
offer wares unavailable elsewhere in the city.
Georgetown has most of the city's antiques deal-
ers, craft shops, and high-style clothing boutiques.

Dupont Circle has some of the same flavor as
Georgetown. Here, too, there is a lively mix of
shops and restaurants, with most of the action
on the major artery of Connecticut Avenue.
There are many book and record stores in the
neighborhood, as well as stores selling coffees,
stationery, and bric-a-brac.

The city's department stores can be found in the
"new" downtown, which is still being built. Its
fulcrum is **Metro Center,** which spans 11th and
12th streets NW along G Street. The Metro
Center subway stop takes you directly into the
basements of downtown's two major department stores, Woodward & Lothrop, familiarly
called "Woodies," and Hecht's. Take the 11th
and G streets exit to Woodies; for Hecht's, follow the signs to the 12th or 13th Street exits.

The new downtown mall, **The Shops at National
Place** (13th and F Sts. NW, tel. 202/783–9090),
takes up three levels, one of which is devoted to
food stands. The Shops is oriented primarily to
younger consumers. This is a good place to drop
off teenagers weary of the Smithsonian and
more in the mood to buy compact discs or T-
shirts. Banana Republic, Victoria's Secret, and
The Sharper Image are three of the catalogue
stores that have outlets here.

Resplendent with marble floors and gilded,
vaulted ceilings, **Union Station** (Massachusetts
Ave. NE, near North Capitol St. on the
Metrorail red line) is now both a working train
station and a mall with three levels of stores, including one level of food stands. Union Station is
full of trendy clothing boutiques, including
Cignal, Chico's, and Montinaro. Other stores

worthy of special mention are Political America and The Nature Company.

Department Stores

Hecht's (12th and G Sts. NW, tel. 202/628–6661). The new downtown Hecht's is bright and spacious, and its sensible groupings and attractive displays of merchandise make shopping relatively easy on the feet and the eyes. The clothes sold here are a mix of conservative and trendy lines, with the men's department assuming increasing importance. Cosmetics, lingerie, and housewares are also strong departments.

Lord & Taylor (5255 Western Ave., tel. 202/362–9600). Lord & Taylor lets other stores be all things to all people, while it focuses on nonutilitarian housewares and classic clothing by such designers as Anne Klein and Ralph Lauren.

Neiman Marcus (Mazza Gallerie, tel. 202/966–9700). If you have to ask how much it costs, you probably shouldn't shop at Neiman Marcus, which caters to the customer who values quality above all.

Woodward & Lothrop (11th and F Sts. NW, tel. 202/347–5300). The largest of the downtown stores, Woodies has eight floors of merchandise that can accommodate just about any need or whim. There are two floors of women's clothing in a variety of style and price ranges, another floor for juniors, one for men, and a large children's department. In addition, just about anything you could need for the home can be found here, including gourmet food.

Specialty Stores

Adams-Morgan Shopping In Adams-Morgan, scattered among the dozens of Latin, Ethiopian, and Caribbean restaurants in this most bohemian of Washington neighborhoods, are a score of the city's most eccentric shops. Adams-Morgan retailing reflects its population—trendy gift shops for the young and affluent, leftist bookstores, vintage clothing, boutiques selling objets d'art (or at least objets), and used furniture that sometimes approaches the antique. It's a minefield of quality, but great fun for the bargain hunter.

Chenonceau Antiques (2314 18th St. NW, tel. 202/667–1651). Two floors of French and American mostly 19th-century pieces selected by a buyer with an eye for the exquisite. Beautiful 19th-century paisley scarves from India and from Scotland. French travel posters from the '30s.

Nice Stuff (2102½ 18th St. NW, no phone). An Adams-Morgan used-furniture shop with a random selection of storage and bedroom furniture from the '20s, '30s, and '40s. Odd bits of kitsch and the occasional great buy. Closed Monday–Wednesday.

Retrospective (2324 18th St. NW, tel. 202/483–8112). A small shop crammed with high-quality furniture and accessories, mostly from the '40s and '50s. Here you can still buy the princess phone that lit up your nightstand in 1962 and the plates your mother served her meat loaf on.

Ruff and Ready (2220 18th St. NW, tel. 202/462–4541). It could be called Adams-Morgan's most venerable used-furniture store except that the word seems so out of place in this jumble of styles and quality. A great selection of estate sale furniture that moves out of the store almost as fast as it moves in—and the prices make the reason clear.

Uniform (2318 18th St. NW, tel. 202/483–4577). The best of the vintage clothing and household accessories shops in Adams-Morgan, an assortment from the '50s and '60s that makes it seem like the entire country transferred to the moon for 20 years.

Antiques **Cherishables** (1608 20th St. NW, tel. 202/785–4087) offers American 18th- and 19th-century furniture and decorative arts, with emphasis on the Federal period.

G.K.S. Bush (2828 Pennsylvania Ave. NW, tel. 202/965–0653). Formal American furniture from the 18th and early 19th centuries, plus related American antiques and works of art.

Marston Luce (1314 21st St. NW, tel. 202/775–9460). The specialty here is American folk art, including quilts, weather vanes, and hooked rugs. There is also furniture and garden furnishings, primarily American, but some English and French as well.

Old Print Gallery (1220 31st St. NW, tel. 202/965-1818). The area's only store specializing in old prints and maps, including Washingtoniana.

Susquehanna (1319 Wisconsin Ave. NW, tel. 202/333-1511). The largest antique shop in Georgetown, specializing in American furniture and paintings.

Books **Chapters** (1512 K St. NW, tel. 202/347-5495). Calling itself a "literary bookstore," Chapters eschews cartoon collections and diet guides, filling its shelves instead with the sort of books that are meant to be read—serious contemporary fiction, classics, and poetry.

The Cheshire Cat (5512 Connecticut Ave. NW, tel. 202/244-3956). A bookstore for children, with a selection of records, cassettes, posters, and books on parenting.

Crown Books (1200 New Hampshire Ave. NW, tel. 202/822-8331. Also at 3131 M St. NW, tel. 202/333-4493; 2020 K St. NW, tel. 202/659-2030; 3335 Connecticut Ave. NW, tel. 202/966-7232; 4301 Connecticut Ave. NW, tel. 202/966-2576; 4400 Jennifer St. NW, tel. 202/966-8784; and 1710 G St. NW, 202/789-2277). This large local chain sells hardback best-sellers at significant discounts.

Olsson's Books & Records (1239 Wisconsin Ave., tel. 202/338-9544. Also at 1307 19th St. NW, tel. 202/785-1133; and 1200 F St. NW, tel. 202/347-3686). With its large and varied collection, this is undoubtedly the area's preeminent general bookstore. Hours vary significantly from store to store.

Crafts and Gifts **The American Hand** (2906 M St. NW, tel. 202/965-3273). One-of-a-kind functional and nonfunctional pieces from America's foremost ceramic artists, plus limited-edition objects for home and office, such as architect-designed dinnerware.

Appalachian Spring (1415 Wisconsin Ave., tel. 202/337-5780, and Union Station, tel. 202/682-0505). Traditional and contemporary crafts, including quilts, jewelry, weavings, pottery, and blown glass.

Fahrney's (1430 G St. NW, tel. 202/628-9525). Fahrney's started out as a pen bar in the Willard

Hotel, a place to fill your fountain pen before embarking on the day's business. Today it offers pens in silver, gold, and lacquer by the world's leading manufacturers.

Indian Craft Shop (1050 Wisconsin Ave., tel. 202/342–3918. Also at Dept. of Interior, 1800 C St. NW, tel. 202/208–4056). Handicrafts, including jewelry, pottery, sand paintings, weavings, and baskets, from a dozen Native American tribal traditions.

Save the Children's Craft Shop (2803 M St. NW, tel. 202/342–8096). Part of a program to help families supplement their income and at the same time preserve their cultural heritage, this store sells crafts from more than 20 countries, including the United States. Wood carvings, masks, weavings, and wall hangings are among the moderately priced offerings.

Jewelry **Charles Schwartz & Son** (Mazza Gallerie, tel. 202/363–5432). A full-service jeweler specializing in precious stones in traditional and modern settings. Fine watches are also offered.

Pampillonia Jewelers (Mazza Gallerie, tel. 202/363–6305. Also at 1213 Connecticut Ave. NW, tel. 202/628–6305). Traditional designs in 18-karat gold and platinum, including many pieces for men.

Kitchenware **Kitchen Bazaar** (4401 Connecticut Ave. NW, tel. 202/244–1550. Also at the Fashion Centre at Pentagon City, 1100 South Hayes St., Arlington, VA, tel. 703/415–5545). This emporium carries just about everything one could possibly need to equip a kitchen.

Little Caledonia (1419 Wisconsin Ave., tel. 202/333–4700). A "Tom Thumb department store" for the home, this old Georgetown store consists of nine rooms crammed with almost 100,000 items, with candles, cards, fabrics, and lamps rounding out the stock of decorative kitchenware.

Leather Goods **Camalier & Buckley** (1141 Connecticut Ave., tel. 202/347–7700. Also at 1365 F St. NW, tel. 202/347–6232). The city's largest collection of briefcases in a variety of skins, plus luggage, desk accessories, stationery, clocks, crystal, and porcelain.

Georgetown Leather Design (3265 M St. NW,

tel. 202/333-9333. Also at 5300 Wisconsin Ave. NW, tel. 202/363-9710; and 1150 Connecticut Ave. NW, tel. 202/223-1855). A full line of leather goods, most of them made for the store, including jackets, briefcases, wallets, gloves, and handbags.

Men's Clothing

Britches of Georgetown (1247 Wisconsin Ave., tel. 202/338-3330. Also at 1219 Connecticut Ave. NW, tel. 202/347-8994). Britches carries an extensive selection of traditional but trend-conscious designs in natural fibers.

Brooks Brothers (1840 L St. NW, tel. 202/659-4650. Also at 5500 Wisconsin Ave. NW, tel. 301/654-8202). The oldest men's store in America, Brooks Brothers has offered traditional formal and casual clothing since 1818. It is the largest men's specialty store in the area and has a small women's department as well.

Hugo Boss (1201 Connecticut Ave., tel. 202/887-5081. Also at 1517 Wisconsin Ave. tel. 202/338-0120; and 5454 Wisconsin Ave. NW, tel. 301/907-7806). The Washington area has the only U.S. collection of clothes from this German designer and manufacturer, noted for his classic fabrics and unique silhouettes.

Men's and Women's Clothing

The Gap (5430 Wisconsin Ave., tel. 202/657-3380. Also at 1217 Connecticut Ave., tel. 202/638-4603; 5215 Wisconsin Ave. NW, tel 202/686-9523; and 1267 Wisconsin Ave. NW, tel. 202/333-2657). Well-designed and well-made jeans, T-shirts, and other casual clothing in natural fibers.

Raleighs (1133 Connecticut Ave., tel. 202/833-0120. Also in Mazza Gallerie, tel. 202/244-6400). A specialty store catering to men and noted for its well-tailored suits, Raleighs also has a small women's department.

Records

Kemp Mill Record Shops (1260 Wisconsin Ave., tel. 202/333-1392. Also at 1517 Connecticut Ave. NW, tel. 202/332-8247; 4304 Connecticut Ave. NW, tel. 202/362-9262; 2459 18th St. NW, tel. 202/387-1011; 1900 L St. NW, tel. 202/223-5310; and 4000 Wisconsin Ave. NW, tel. 202/364-9704). This local chain store concentrates on popular music (New Age is a particular specialty) and keeps its prices low. Also at several locations in the suburbs.

Tower Records (2000 Pennsylvania Ave. NW, tel. 202/331–2400). With 16,000 square feet of selling space, Tower offers the area's best selection of music in all categories. Open daily until midnight.

Shoes   **Bally** (1020 Connecticut Ave. NW, tel. 202/429–0604). The Swiss manufacturer of high-quality leather goods is expanding its line of women's shoes, but the focus is still on footwear for men, primarily European-style loafers. The store also sells handbags, briefcases, and belts.

Shoe Scene (1330 Connecticut Ave. NW, tel. 202/659–2194). A good selection of moderately priced, fashionable shoes for women.

Women's Clothing   **Ann Taylor** (1720 K St. NW, tel. 202/466–3544. Also at 3222 M St. NW, tel. 202/338–5290; 5300 Wisconsin Ave. NW, tel. 202/244–1940; and Union Station, tel. 202/371–8010). Sophisticated fashions for the woman who has broken out of the dress-for-success mold. Ann Taylor also has an excellent shoe department.

Benetton (3108 M St. NW, tel. 202/333–7839. Also at 1234 Wisconsin Ave. NW, tel. 202/337–0632; 1350 Connecticut Ave. NW, tel. 202/785–4607; and Union Station, tel. 202/289–8422). A line of Italian sportswear, primarily knits, in bright colors and mix-and-unmatch patterns.

The Limited (Georgetown Park, tel. 202/342–5150. Also at 1331 Pennsylvania Ave. NW, tel. 202/628–8221; 1024 Connecticut Ave. NW, tel. 202/955–5710; Mazza Gallerie, tel. 202/244–2200; and Union Station, tel. 202/682–0416). Moderately priced casual clothing with European flair. The store also has suburban locations.

4 Dining

Introduction

by Deborah Papier

It is often said of Washington's weather that if you don't like it, all you have to do is wait a minute. The same applies to the city's restaurant scene. Every week, at least, a restaurant opens or closes or changes ownership, chef, or menu. In the space of a month whole categories of cuisine can appear or disappear.

This can be frustrating, since it means that a restaurant you have enjoyed visiting—or were looking forward to visiting—may be transformed or gone when you arrive. But it's also exhilarating, since there are always new places to discover.

And although a particular restaurant may falter or fall, in general, Washington's restaurants are getting better and better. In the last few years Italian restaurants have come to rival French establishments, which for a long time set the standard in fine dining. There has also been an explosion of the kind of cooking usually called New American. Its practitioners don't much like that label, but whatever you call the cuisine, it has brought considerable style and energy to the area's restaurant scene.

Despite the dearth of ethnic neighborhoods in Washington and the corresponding lack of the kinds of restaurant districts found in many cities, you *can* find almost any type of food here, from Nepalese to Salvadoran to Ethiopian.

Highly recommended restaurants are indicated by a star ★.

Category	Cost*
Very Expensive	over $35
Expensive	$25–$35
Moderate	$15–$25
Inexpensive	under $15

average cost of a 3-course dinner, per person, excluding drinks, service, and (9%) sales tax

Adams-Morgan

American   **Belmont Kitchen.** Dining outside on a warm
spring night at this popular Adams-Morgan
neighborhood spot is one of the best ways to get
a flavor of the rich street life of the neighborhood. The kitchen specializes in upside-down
pizzas and simple, well-prepared grilled fish
and meats. A low-calorie three-course dinner is
always on the menu. Parking in Adams-Morgan
is always difficult. *2400 18th St. NW, tel. 202/
667–1200. Reservations advised. Dress: casual.
DC, MC, V. Moderate.*

Caribbean   **Fish, Wings & Tings.** You don't go to this wild-
and-woolly restaurant for a quiet meal, any
more than you put on a reggae record for background music. This Caribbean café (or *mini
kafe,* according to the menu) is the brilliantly idiosyncratic creation of a husband-and-wife
team. She's from Jamaica and works in the
kitchen. He's a Panamanian with dreadlocks
who keeps a semblance of order in the tiny dining room, which is barely able to contain the
crowds that wait for carryout or for one of the
few tables. The menu includes stewed oxtail and
curry goat, but most people come here for the
curry-ginger chicken wings, or the jerk (barbecued) thighs. Marinated and grilled rainbow
trout is another popular item from the regular
menu, which is supplemented by two or three
daily specials, usually poultry or fish. *2418 18th
St. NW, tel. 202/234–0322. Reservations not accepted. Dress: casual. AE. Closed Sun. Inexpensive.*

Ethiopian   **Meskerem.** Adams-Morgan may well have more
Ethiopian restaurants than Ethiopia itself—
about a dozen in a three-block stretch of 18th
Street. While all of them have virtually identical
menus, Meskerem is distinctive for its bright,
appealingly decorated dining room. Another attractive feature: The restaurant has a balcony
where you can eat Ethiopian-style—seated on
the floor on leather cushions, with large woven
baskets for tables. But whether it is served atop
baskets or on conventional tables, an Ethiopian
meal is definitely exotic. There is no silverware;
instead, the food is scooped up with *injera,* a
spongy flat bread that also does duty as the plat-

ter on which the meal is presented. The country's main dish is the *watt*, or stew, which may be made with chicken, lamb, beef, or shrimp in either a spicy or a mild sauce. Several vegetarian watts are also available. *2434 18th St. NW, tel. 202/462–4100. Reservations advised. Dress: casual but neat. AE, DC, MC, V. Closed lunch Mon.–Thurs. Inexpensive.*

French **La Fourchette.** Located on a block in Adams-Morgan where new restaurants are opening almost weekly and closing just as fast, La Fourchette has stayed in business for over a decade by offering good bistro food at reasonable prices. Most of the menu consists of daily specials, but you can pretty much count on finding bouillabaisse and rabbit on the list. The most popular entrées on the regular menu are the hearty veal and lamb shanks. La Fourchette also looks the way a bistro should, with an exposed brick wall, tin ceiling, bentwood chairs, and quasi–post-impressionist murals. *2429 18th St. NW, tel. 202/332–3077. Reservations advised. Dress: casual but neat. AE, DC, MC, V. Closed lunch Sat. and Sun. Moderate.*

Italian **I Matti.** Owned by chef Roberto Donna of the highly praised Galileo, I Matti is a much less formal but just as popular restaurant. The stark modern setting and the crowds of well-dressed young people somehow encapsulate Adams-Morgan trendiness. It's possible to order anything from a pizza to a multi-course meal from the large menu. The breads, including the foccacia and the pizzas, are delicious. Osso buco is a good bet from the inconsistent kitchen. *2436 18th St. NW., tel. 202/462–8444. Reservations advised. Dress: casual. AE, DC, MC, V. Moderate.*

Capitol Hill

American **America.** A Washington outpost of owner Michael Weinstein's America in New York, Union Station's America is installed in the west front of the station in the space which was, before the remodeling, occupied by the men's room. The space has been opened up and transformed into a lively and attractive bar and restaurant. The disparate design elements—WPA-style murals,

Washington Dining

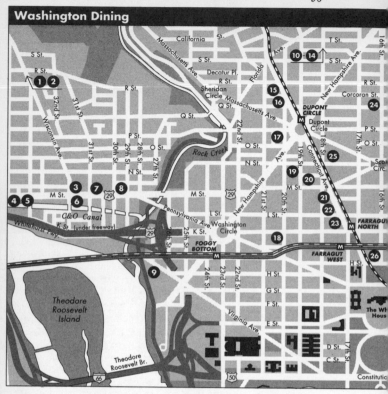

America, **34**

American Cafe, **3**

Austin Grill, **1**

Bamiyan, **4**

Belmont Kitchen, **13**

Bice, **32**

Bistro Francais, **6**

Bombay Club, **26**

Duke Zeibert's, **23**

Fish, Wings & Tings, **12**

Georgetown Seafood Grill, **7**

Geppetto, **8**

I Matti, **14**

i Ricchi, **19**

Jean-Louis at the Watergate Hotel, **9**

La Colline, **33**

La Fourchette, **11**

Le Lion D'Or, **21**

McPherson Grill, **27**

Meskerem, **10**

The Monocle, **36**

Notte Luna, **28**

Occidental and Occidental Grill, **30**

Odeon, **15**

Old Ebbitt Grill, **29**

The Palm, **20**

Prime Rib, **18**

Sala Thai, **17**

701 Pennsylvania Avenue, **31**

Sfuzzi, **35**

Skewers, **24**

Sushi-Ko, **2**

Tabard Inn, **25**

Tandoor, **5**

Twenty-One Federal, **22**

Vincenzo, **16**

Western landscapes, aluminum outlines of states, superheroes—seem to be united only by the fact that they all somehow pertain to America, but the space itself is so impressive that they all seem to cohere. The menu is enormous, with nearly four square feet of regular offerings ranging from Kansas City steaks to Minnesota scrambled eggs, New Orleans muffalata sandwiches to New Mexico–style pasta, Jersey pork chops to San Diego fish tacos. The kitchen has its successes and failures—a good general rule is "the simpler the better." Desserts are good, and service is pleasant though chaotic. *Union Station, 50 Massachusetts Ave. NE (Union Station Metro stop), tel. 202/682–9555. Reservations advised. Dress: casual but neat. AE, DC, MC, V. Parking validated in Union Station lot. Moderate.*

The Monocle. The bar at the Monocle is probably the closest thing on the Hill to the smoke-filled political hangout from the movies, but in truth, nobody smokes much anymore, and drinking is on the decline too. But The Monocle is still a hangout, probably the best place for spotting senators at lunch and dinner; management keeps members of congress informed on when it's time to vote. In other words, nobody really goes to The Monocle for the food even though it may be one of the most underrated restaurants in Washington. The cooking, American cuisine with a Continental touch, is quite good and moderately priced considering its clientele. Seafood is a specialty; try the crabcakes, and take advantage of the lobster specials. *107 D St. NE, tel. 202/546–4488. Reservations advised. Jacket and tie advised. AE, DC, MC, V. Closed Sat. lunch and Sun. Expensive.*

French **La Colline.** Even before Washington became a
★ contender in the U.S. restaurant ring, it did have its heavyweight chefs, such as Robert Gréault, originally of Le Bagatelle. For the past nine years Gréault has worked to make La Colline into one of the city's best French restaurants and the best of any type on Capitol Hill. When it first opened, La Colline was also one of the city's great bargains. That's no longer the case; unless you order the special fixed-price dinner, a meal at La Colline is likely to be

pricey. But it's worth it. The menu changes daily, and it seems always to strike the perfect balance between innovation and tradition. The emphasis is on seafood, with offerings ranging from simple grilled preparations to fricassees and gratins with imaginative sauces. The non-seafood menu usually offers duck with an orange or cassis sauce and veal with chanterelles. Desserts are superb, as is the wine list. *400 N. Capitol St. (3 blocks from Union Station Metro stop), tel. 202/737-0400. Reservations required. Jacket and tie advised. AE, DC, MC, V. Closed lunch Sat. and Sun. Free parking in underground lot. Expensive.*

Italian **Sfuzzi.** Since its opening in 1989, this Italian restaurant in the northeast corner of Union Station has been one of the most popular spots in town, mixing Hill politicos and staffers with Washington's young fashionable set. The interior is strikingly attractive; trompe l'oeil murals create an Italian fantasy of classical ruins and crumbling frescoes. No other dining room in Washington has a better view of the Capitol dome than the upstairs at Sfuzzi, and its private dining room has a spectacular view of the main hall of the station. And the care with which the restaurant has been designed is generally matched by the attention given to the food. The house-baked breads are flavorful and firm textured. In this salad-poor city it's refreshing to find salads that are interestingly conceived and carefully prepared. The best items on the menu, however, are the pizzas, which may be ordered as an appetizer to be shared or as a main course. The crust is crisp, yeasty, and flavorful, and the toppings immaculately fresh and varied. Grilled foods are well prepared. The addictive house drink is called a "Sfuzzi," a sort of frozen Bellini. *Union Station, 50 Massachusetts Ave. NE (Union Station Metro stop), tel. 202/842-4141. Reservations required. Jacket and tie advised. AE, DC, MC, V. Parking validated in Union Station garage. Expensive.*

Downtown

American **The Palm.** Food trends come and go, but the Palm pays no attention; it offers the same he-man food it always has—gargantuan steaks and lobsters, several kinds of potatoes, New York cheesecake. The staff's been packing them in for 17 years with this kind of fare, and they're not about to let the calorie- and cholesterol-counters spoil the party. The look of the restaurant is basement basic—acoustic ceiling tiles, wooden fans—nothing to distract one from the serious business of chowing down. In addition to the beef and lobsters it is famous for, the Palm also offers lamb chops, two veal and two poultry entrées, fresh fish, and linguini with clam sauce. *1225 19th St. NW, tel. 202/293–9091. Reservations advised. Dress: casual but neat. AE, DC, MC, V. Closed Sat. lunch and Sun. Very Expensive.*

★ **Prime Rib.** Despite its name, the Prime Rib is no longer really a steakhouse. In response to the increasing popularity of seafood, it now devotes half its menu to fish and shellfish, some of it shipped express from Florida. The most popular of the seafood dishes is the imperial crab, made only of jumbo lump-crabmeat; the crab imperial is also stuffed in a two-pound lobster. The aged beef from Chicago includes a steak au poivre in addition to New York strip, porterhouse, filet mignon, and the restaurant's namesake, for which you might need to reserve ahead. Also served are simple preparations of veal, pork, lamb, and chicken. Prime Rib is an unusually attractive restaurant; its black walls, leather chairs, and leopardskin print rugs give it a timeless sophistication. *2020 K St. NW (1 block from Farragut West Metro stop), tel. 202/466–8811. Reservations advised. Jacket and tie required. AE, DC, MC, V. Closed Sat. lunch and Sun. Very Expensive.*

Duke Zeibert's. At lunch, this 450-seat restaurant is filled with regulars who come to talk sports with Duke and eat heartily from a menu that essentially hasn't changed in 39 years—boiled beef and chicken in a pot, deli sandwiches, and specials like corned beef and cabbage. At dinner, only the front room is used, and the restaurant becomes a different place, with couples and families replacing the deal makers. In the evening the signature chicken and beef in a pot are still available, but the menu leans more toward broiler items like lamb chops and sirloin, not to mention two dishes for which the restaurant is famous—prime rib and crab cakes. This may also be the only place in town where you can get chicken soup with matzo balls, and potato pancakes. *1050 Connecticut Ave. NW (on the mezzanine of the Washington Square Building at Farragut North Metro stop), tel. 202/466–3730. Reservations required. Jacket and tie advised. AE, DC, MC, V. Closed lunch Sun. Closed Sun. during July and Aug. Validated parking at Washington Square lot. Expensive.*

Old Ebbitt Grill. It doesn't have the charm of the old Old Ebbitt, which was urban-renewed out of existence, but this incarnation of Washington's longest-lived restaurant is obviously doing something right—it does more business than any other eating place in town. People flock here to drink at the several bars, which seem to go on for miles, and to enjoy carefully prepared bar food that includes buffalo chicken wings, hamburgers, and reuben sandwiches. But this is not just a place for casual nibbling; the Old Ebbitt offers serious diners homemade pastas and a list of daily specials, with the emphasis on fish dishes like Shenandoah trout in a champagne sauce. Despite the crowds, the restaurant never feels crowded, thanks to its well-spaced, comfortable booths. *675 15th St. NW (2 blocks from Metro Center Metro stop), tel. 202/347–4800. Reservations advised. Dress: casual but neat. AE, DC, MC, V. Moderate.*

French
★ **Jean-Louis at the Watergate Hotel.** A showcase for the cooking of Jean-Louis Palladin, who was the youngest chef in France ever to be recognized with two stars by the Michelin raters, this small restaurant is often cited as one of the best in the United States. The contemporary French fare is based on regional American ingredients—crawfish from Louisiana, wild mushrooms from Oregon, game from Texas—combined in innovative ways. There are two limited-choice fixed-price dinners: one with five courses, for $75 per person, the other with six courses (the additional course is a foie-gras dish), for $90. There is also a pre-theater menu of four courses for $38, designed for but not limited to those attending the nearby Kennedy Center. In general, the first course is a soup or terrine; corn soup with oysters and lobster que-

nelles is a signature offering. Next comes a shellfish preparation, perhaps a potato stuffed with lobster mousseline; then a fish course, such as snapper with braised cabbage; and last, a meat dish, perhaps rack of lamb with artichoke ragout. The wine cellar is said to be the largest on the East Coast. *2650 Virginia Ave. NW (downstairs in the Watergate Hotel, which can be entered from Virginia or New Hampshire aves., 3 blocks from Foggy Bottom Metro stop), tel. 202/298–4488. Reservations required. Jacket and tie required. AE, DC, MC, V. Closed lunch, Sun., and the last 2 weeks in Aug. Validated parking. Very Expensive.*

★ **Le Lion D'Or.** Other French restaurants may flirt with fads, but this one sticks to the classics—or at any rate the neo-classics—and does them so well that its popularity remains undiminished year after year. Aside from the owner's collection of faience and the abudant floral arrangements, the decor doesn't do much to entertain the eye. But the palate is another story. This is the sort of food that makes the French posture of cultural superiority almost defensible: lobster soufflé, crêpes with oysters and caviar, ravioli with foie gras, salmon with crayfish, roast pigeon with mushrooms, lamb with green peppercorns. The long list of daily specials can get rather confusing unless you take notes while the waiter recites them. But don't forget to place an order for a dessert soufflé—it will leave you breathless. *1150 Connecticut Ave. NW (at Farragut North Metro stop), tel. 202/296–7972. Reservations required. Jacket and tie required. AE, DC, MC, V. Closed Sat. lunch and Sun. Free parking in lot next door at dinner. Very Expensive.*

Indian **The Bombay Club.** Located just a block from the White House, the Bombay Club tries to re-create for tired Executive Office bureaucrats, power lawyers, and jounalists the kind of solace they might have found in a private club had they been 19th-century British colonialists in India rather than the late 20th-century Washingtonians. It's a very beautiful restaurant. The bar, which serves hot hors d'oeuvres at cocktail hour, is furnished with rattan chairs and paneled with dark wood. The dining room, with potted palms

and a bright blue ceiling above white plaster
moldings, is elegant and decorous. The menu includes unusual seafood specialties like lobster
Malabar and a large number of vegetarian
dishes, but the real standout is on the appetizer
list: the Club Scallops will not fail you. *815 Connecticut Ave. NW, tel. 202/659–3727. Reservations advised. Jacket and tie advised. AE, DC,
MC, V.*

International **701 Pennsylvania Avenue.** This sleek new restaurant features an eclectic, international cuisine
drawn from Italy, France, Asia, and the Americas. You might start your meal with an Indian
appetizer of crab masala with tomatoes and cumin cream, progress to a Mexican fish dish of
pescado pibil with chipotle chili, steamed in banana leaves; and finish with an Italian almond-
and-cherry tart. The restaurant's Caviar
Lounge offers caviar from Beluga at $55 a ser-
ving to Louisiana "Choupiquet Royale" at $8.50;
smoked fish; Russian specialties; and 18 different vodkas. One of the most attractive features
of 701 Pennsylvania Avenue is that it is a restaurant which is open relatively late in a town which
by and large closes early, that is, until midnight
Monday through Wednesday and until 2 AM
Thursday through Saturday. A supper menu is
available until closing time. *701 Pennsylvania
Ave. NW, tel. 202/393–0701. Reservations advised. Dress: casual but neat. AE, DC, MC, V.
Closed Sun. Valet parking for dinner. Expensive.*

Italian **Bice.** Bice, which followed its successful 1987
New York opening with additional locations in
Chicago and Beverly Hills, traces its roots to a
trattoria in Tuscany opened by owner Roberto
Ruggeri's mother in 1926. In 1939 she moved the
restaurant to its present location in Milan,
where it became a popular dining spot for the international fashion trade. Washington's Bice,
like the other American locations, is designed
by New York interior designer Adam Tihany,
who uses design elements—wood, brass, warm
lighting, and art deco details—suggested by the
original in Milan. The large menu, which
changes daily, features Milanese and Northern
Italian specialities such as risotto verdi with
mascarpone cheese and spinach, and a classic

breaded veal cutlet alla Milanese. Pasta dishes, featuring hand-made pastas, might include lobster in a fresh tomato and basil sauce or fettuccine with wild mushrooms and chives. *601 Pennsylvania Ave. NW, tel. 202/638–2423. Reservations advised. Jacket and tie advised. AE, DC, MC, V. Closed Sat. and Sun. lunch. Very Expensive.*

i Ricchi. Every once in a while a new restaurant opens that makes even the most level-headed food critics swoon. Two years ago it was i Ricchi, which features the earthy cuisine of the Tuscany region of Italy. There are two menus, one for spring and summer, one for fall and winter. The spring list includes such offerings as rolled pork and rabbit roasted in wine and fresh herbs, and skewered shrimp, while winter brings grilled goat chops and spare ribs. But whatever the calendar says, it always feels like spring in this airy dining room, which is decorated with terra cotta tiles, cream-colored archways, and floral frescoes. *1220 19th St. NW, tel. 202/835–0459. Reservations required. Jacket and tie advised. AE, DC, MC, V. Closed Sat. lunch and Sun. Expensive.*

Notte Luna. Chef Jeff Tunks, whose inventive cooking at The River Club in Georgetown has received wide praise, now divides his time between The River Club and Notte Luna, a glitzy new downtown Italian restaurant. The dining room is dramatic in black and neon; the kitchen, with a wood-burning pizza oven, is open; and the food is informal yet ambitious. The menu offers the Italian-restaurant staples of pasta, pizza, and veal dishes, but at Notte Luna the ordinary often has an unexpected twist. You can order your pizza topped with gravlax or duck confit or your pasta with smoked salmon. Desserts are spectacular. *809 15th St. NW, tel. 202/408–9500. Reservations advised. Dress: casual but neat. AE, DC, MC, V. Closed Sat. and Sun. lunch. Valet parking at dinner. Moderate.*

New American
★ **Occidental and Occidental Grill.** The historic 1906 Occidental restaurant, which re-opened in 1987 after a 16-year hiatus, is now two separate restaurants. Upstairs is the formal restaurant, called simply Occidental; downstairs is the small, casual grill room. Both are preeminent

among the city's New American restaurants, but the Occidental management prefers to consider the establishments simply American, with the emphasis on Chesapeake Bay seafood. The small list of offerings upstairs changes seasonally but always includes a steak (perhaps a filet sautéed with artichokes and wild mushrooms), a veal dish (perhaps stuffed with fresh mozzarella and garlic purée), and various preparations of crabmeat and scallops. The Grill menu changes frequently, but you can count on chicken, fish, and steak as grilled options (the steak might be served with mustard seed, thyme, and bourbon sauce), plus salads and sandwiches. The upstairs room has parquet floors, red velvet booths, and etched glass; the downstairs is done in dark wood and brown banquettes, with 900 photos of the formerly famous animating the walls. *1475 Pennsylvania Ave. NW (3 blocks from Metro Center Metro Stop), tel. 202/783–1475. Reservations advised for the Occidental, but only accepted for certain times at the Grill; count on a long wait otherwise. Jacket and tie advised upstairs. AE, DC, MC, V. Occidental closed Sat. lunch and Sun.; Grill closed Sun. Occidental, Very Expensive; Grill, Expensive.*

★ **Twenty-One Federal.** Offering New American cuisine in a sophisticated setting, Twenty-One Federal is one of the city's hottest restaurants. The menu changes seasonally but always includes a spit-roasted chicken; lamb, pheasant, and rabbit are also prepared on the rotisserie. The New England–born chef has a way with seafood, as exemplified in his grilled oysters and pancetta. But meat eaters will find much to satisfy them as well—such dishes as beef in a marrow-shallot crust, and a lamb plate that includes a rack chop, a loin stuffed with veal, and a grilled, butterflied slice of leg. A pianist plays nightly in the large dining room, which is decorated primarily in black and gray, with marble tiles and brass gridwork adding a touch of class. *1736 L St. NW (½ block from Farragut North Metro stop), tel. 202/331–9771. Reservations advised. Jacket and tie advised. AE, DC, MC, V. Closed Sat. lunch and Sun. Free valet parking at dinner. Very Expensive.*

McPherson Grill. It is said that nothing is riskier than opening a new restaurant. But there does seem to be one sure-fire formula for success in the restaurant business: Find a central location, hire decorators who know how to fill a room with light, install a grill, and concentrate on seafood. At the McPherson Grill, the seafood includes what may be the most sublime salmon in town—a grilled or steamed fillet with lobster, roast corn, and rosemary butter. Other fish preparations you might encounter on the seasonal menu are tuna steak with coriander, wilted greens, and red bell pepper coulis; and swordfish with dill-butter. Meat possibilities include grilled chicken with cumin, lamb steak with olives and goat cheese, and pork chops with charred tomato relish. Desserts are homey: peach cobbler, coconut-custard pie. *950 15th St. NW (1 block from McPherson Square Metro stop), tel. 202/638–0950. Reservations suggested at lunch. Dress: casual but neat. AE, DC, MC, V. Closed Sat. lunch and Sun.; closed Sat. and Sun. during Aug. Expensive.*

Dupont Circle

Italian
★
Vincenzo. Vincenzo has relaxed somewhat since its early days, when it was so determined to be authentically Italian that it refused to serve butter with the bread. Butter is now available (on request), and the once exclusively seafood menu has been supplemented with a few meat dishes—game in autumn, pork in winter, lamb in spring. But it is still a restaurant for purists who appreciate its commitment to finding the best fish it can and serving it as simply as possible. Dinner is fixed-price and includes an appetizer, first course, main dish, side dish, and dessert; lunch is à la carte. Along with its enlarged menu, Vincenzo has expanded its dining space, adding a glassed-in courtyard. Already light and airy, Vincenzo now more than ever seems touched by Mediterranean breezes. *1601 20th St. NW (1 block from Q St. exit of Dupont Circle Metro stop), tel. 202/667–0047. Reservations advised. Dress: casual but neat. AE, DC, MC, V. No lunch weekend. Very Expensive.*

Odeon. Like the country as a whole, Washington is in the midst of a fourth Italian invasion. First to arrive were the red-tablecloth southern-Italian restaurants. Then came white-tablecloth northern-Italian places, which teetered on the borderline of French. Third, and still moving in, are the elegant and authentic regional-Italian restaurants. Last have come the new-wave Italians, slick pizza-and-pasta parlors whose food is more or less true to its roots, but whose sensibility is strictly New York. Odeon is a preeminent example of this type. On the surface Odeon seems all surface—glossy to the point of being almost intimidating. But amid all the glass and marble and the resultant din is some very good food. Pasta and pizza dough are made in house and topped with first-class ingredients. In addition, there is a good list of grilled dishes, and specials change every two weeks. *1714 Connecticut Ave. NW (2 blocks from Q Street exit of Dupont Circle Metro stop), tel. 202/328–6228. Reservations advised on weekdays, not accepted on weekends. Dress: casual but neat. AE, MC, V. Closed lunch Sat. and Sun. Moderate.*

Middle Eastern

Skewers. Depending on your point of view, Skewers is an American restaurant with a strong Middle Eastern influence or an avant-garde Middle Eastern restaurant. In either case, it offers fresh, flavorful meals at reasonable prices. This is where Ralph Nader eats both lunch and dinner, so you know you're getting healthful food and good value. As the name implies, Skewers's specialty is kebabs. The lamb with eggplant and the chicken with roasted pepper are the most popular, but filet mignon and shrimp are equally tasty. For those wanting less meat—perhaps to leave room for scrumptious desserts like Key-lime pie or chocolate cake— mini kebobs are available, either served with pita bread or in a salad. Just as the menu favors imagination over ostentation, so does Skewers's decor, which uses a few lengths of shimmering cloth to create an Arabian Nights fantasy. *1633 P St. NW (½ blocks from the Dupont Circle Metro stop), tel. 202/387–7400. Reservations advised on weekends. Dress: casual. AE, DC, MC, V. Moderate.*

New American

Tabard Inn. With its artfully artless decor, absent-minded waiters, and quasi–health-food menu, the Tabard is an idiosyncratic restaurant that has a devoted clientele of baby-boomers with '60s values and '80s incomes. The lounge looks like a garage sale waiting to happen, and the two dining rooms are likewise somewhat shabby. But the courtyard may be Washington's prettiest outdoor eatery, and the Tabard's New American cuisine, although it doesn't always quite come off, is fresh and interesting. The Tabard raises much of its produce, without pesticides, on its own farm; meat is additive-free. Most of the menu changes daily; complicated preparations of fish are a specialty. Desserts are not to be missed. And in a city where finding a good breakfast—or any breakfast at all—can be a major challenge, the Tabard is outstanding for the quantity and quality of its offerings. *1739 N St. NW (5 blocks from Dupont Circle or Farragut North Metro stops), tel. 202/833–2668. Reservations advised. Dress: casual. MC, V. Very Expensive.*

Thai　**Sala Thai.** This is not the sort of Thai restaurant where you go for the burn; the Sala Thai will make the food as spicy as you wish, but the chef is interested in flavor, not fire. Among the subtly seasoned offerings are *panang goong* (shrimp in curry-peanut sauce), chicken sautéed with ginger and pineapple, and flounder with a choice of four sauces. The *Pad Thai* P Street is an exceptional treatment of that signature dish, which consists of noodles with shrimp and bean sprouts in a peanut sauce. Sala Thai is decorated in the currently fashionable minimalist style, but colored lights take the harsh edges off its industrial look. *2016 P St. NW (3 blocks from Dupont Circle Metro stop), tel. 202/872–1144. Reservations accepted. Dress: casual but neat. AE, DC, MC, V. Closed Sun. lunch. Inexpensive.*

Georgetown

Afghani　**Bamiyan.** Because not many people are vacationing in Afghanistan these days, Afghani food is largely unknown in the West. That's a pity, because the country's cuisine is quite appealing, unusual enough to be interesting but not so strange as to be intimidating. Bamiyan is the oldest and arguably the best Afghanian restaurant in the area, even though it does look like a motel that has seen better days. Kebabs—of chicken, beef, or lamb—are succulent. More adventurous souls should try the *quabili palow* (lamb with saffron rice, carrots, and raisins) or the *aushak* (dumplings with scallions, meat sauce, and yogurt). For a side vegetable, order the sautéed pumpkin; it will make you forget every other winter squash dish you've ever had. *3320 M St. NW, tel. 202/338–1896. Reservations accepted. Dress: casual. AE, MC, V. Closed lunch. Moderate.*

American **Georgetown Seafood Grill.** For years you would never have guessed that the Chesapeake Bay was in Washington's backyard, so landlocked were the kitchens in most of the city's restaurants. That's changed, but the city still has very few of the sort of restaurants you expect to find near water—unpretentious places where your oysters are shucked in front of you. The Georgetown Seafood Grill does not have unpretentious prices, but in every other respect it is the perfect seafood eatery. It has an appropriately weathered visage—old tilework and exposed brick decorated with nautical photographs— and its menu casts a wide net. There are four or five kinds of oysters at the raw bar, plus clams, spiced shrimp, and crab claws. Crab cakes are made with jumbo lump-meat and no filler, and soft shell crabs are served in season. On weekends you can order steamed lobsters, and each night you can choose among about seven fish specials—everything from fried catfish to broiled red snapper with macadamia pesto. *3063 M St. NW, tel. 202/333–7038. Reservations accepted for large parties. Dress: casual but neat. AE, DC, MC, V. Expensive.*

American Café. Thirteen years ago someone had the bright idea of opening a Georgetown restaurant that would serve fresh, healthy food—but not health food—at affordable prices in a casual but sophisticated environment. And so the American Café empire, which now numbers 15 restaurants in the Washington area, was born. Sandwiches, such as the namesake roast beef on a humongous croissant, are still the mainstay of the café, with salads and nibbles rounding off the regular menu. But the list of specials, which changes every two weeks, offers intriguing possibilities for those wanting a larger meal.

There's always a fresh fish, a seafood pie, a chicken dish, and barbecued ribs. Weekend brunches offer temptations like strawberry-banana-nut waffles and stuffed French toast. *1211 Wisconsin Ave. NW (also at 227 Massachusetts Ave. NE, tel. 202/547–8500; 1331 Pennsylvania Ave. NW, tel. 202/833–3434; 1200 19th St. NW, tel. 202/223–2121; and 5252 Wisconsin Ave. NW, tel. 202/363–5400), tel. 202/944–9464. Reservations accepted only for large parties. Dress: casual. AE, DC, MC, V. Inexpensive.*

French **Bistro Français.** A longtime fixture on M Street, this French country restaurant is a favorite among the city's chefs. What do the professionals order when they want to eat someone else's cooking? The Minute Steak Maitre d'Hotel, a sirloin with herb butter, accompanied by french fries. Among amateur eaters, the big draw is the rotisserie chicken. While the Bistro excels at such simple fare, it also does well with the more complicated dishes it offers on the extensive list of daily specials, such as supreme of salmon with cauliflower mousse and beurre blanc. The restaurant is divided into two parts, the café side and the more formal dining room. Both have the same comfortable, lived-in look, but the café menu includes sandwiches and omelets in addition to the entrées. The Bistro also offers fixed-price lunches and early- and late-night dinner specials and stays open until 3 AM on weekdays, 4 AM on weekends. *3128 M St. NW, tel. 202/338–3830. Reservations advised. Dress: casual but neat. AE, DC, MC, V. Moderate.*

Indian **Tandoor.** The crucible of Indian cuisine is the *tandoor*, a charcoal-burning clay oven. Meat is cooked on skewers held upright by the coals, and bread is baked directly on the oven walls. This namesake restaurant was the first in town to install a tandoor and consequently the first to give area diners a taste of the real India. The ovens are still rare in town (the fire department doesn't much like them), which means the Tandoor has retained its popularity among aficionados of Indian food. Chicken, lamb filet, and minced lamb, beef, and shrimp are available from the oven, as is a combination platter. The tandoor-cooked meats are also used in a variety of curries, with chicken tikka masala one of the best. This restaurant is not as luxurious as some of the newer Indian restaurants, but its prints of Indian dancers and orange tablecloths make it cheerful. *3316 M St. NW, tel. 202/333–3376, and 2623 Connecticut Ave. NW, tel. 202/483–1115. Reservations advised. Dress: casual but neat. AE, DC, MC, V. Moderate.*

Italian **Geppetto.** Although in most parts of Washington you can choose among half a dozen establishments eager to deliver a pizza to your home or hotel, people still wait in line for pizza at Geppetto—a clear indication that the restaurant delivers quality. The pizza here comes in either a thick- or a thin-crust version. There's also a white pizza (cheese, garlic, and shallot; no tomato sauce) and a geppino, which is essentially a pizza sandwich. Geppetto also serves homemade pastas, several veal and chicken entrées, and a half dozen sandwiches. Named after the creator of Pinocchio and decorated with puppets and cuckoo clocks, this is a good restaurant for children, as long as they can be persuaded to look, not touch. *2917 M St. NW, tel. 202/333–2602. No reservations. Dress: casual. AE, DC, MC, V. Inexpensive.*

Japanese **Sushi-Ko.** This was Washington's first sushi bar, and 12 years later it continues to hold its own against the competition. In addition to the à la carte items and assortments of sushi and sashimi, which vary according to the availability of fish that meets Sushi-Ko's stringent standards for freshness, the menu includes seafood and vegetable tempuras, fish teriyaki, and udonsuki (noodles with seafood and vegetables). Sushi novices might want to test the waters by ordering tuna or yellowtail as an appetizer, followed by one of the cooked dishes. Those looking for more exotic fare will find it on the back of the menu—printed in Japanese, but your waiter will translate. *2309 Wisconsin Ave. NW, tel. 202/333–4187. Reservations advised. Dress: casual but neat. AE, MC, V. Closed Mon. and weekend lunch. Moderate.*

Tex-Mex **Austin Grill.** Even before the 1988 election put a
★ Texan, of sorts, into the White House, Washington was big on Tex-Mex cooking—one of the

city's hot-ticket social events is the annual congressional chili-off. But Washington didn't have a Tex-Mex restaurant of note until the opening of the Austin Grill, a small, lively spot in upper Georgetown whose popularity is well deserved. The Austin has a food-smoker out back, where ribs are prepared for dinner. The mesquite grill is always in operation, turning out fajitas and grilled fish and providing the starting point for what the Austin claims is the best chili in town—made with cubed meat, not ground, unadulterated by beans. With its multicolored booths, the restaurant looks like a post-modern diner; a bright mural adds to the cheerful effect. Waiters are friendly and efficient, a rare combination. *2404 Wisconsin Ave. NW, tel. 202/337–8080. No reservations. Dress: casual. AE, MC, V. Closed Mon. lunch. Inexpensive.*

5 Lodging

Introduction

by Jan Ziegler

A freelance writer and editor, D.C. resident Jan Ziegler contributes frequently to national publications.

The nation's capital has been riding a hotel boom for more than a decade. Between 1976 and 1988, 49 new hotels were built, and it's estimated that more than 2,000 additional hotel rooms will open over the next few years. As a result, visitors who plan to spend the night, a week, or a month in D.C. can expect variety as well as quantity. Hostelries include grand hotels with glorious histories, quiet Victorian inns, the hotel and motel chains common to every American city, and small independently operated hotels that offer little more than good location, a smile, and a comfortable, clean place to lay your head.

Because Washington is an international city, nearly all hotel staffs are multilingual. All hotels in the Expensive and Very Expensive categories have concierges; some in the Moderate group do, too. All of the hotels here are air-conditioned. All the large hotels and many of the smaller ones offer meeting facilities and special features for business travelers, ranging from state-of-the-art teleconferencing equipment to modest conference rooms with outside catering.

To find reasonably priced accommodations in small guest houses and private homes, contact either of the following bed-and-breakfast services: **Bed 'n' Breakfast Ltd. of Washington, D.C.** (Box 12011, Washington, D.C. 20005, tel. 202/328-3510) or **Bed and Breakfast League, Ltd.,** (3639 Van Ness St., Washington, D.C. 20008, tel. 202/363-7767).

Unless otherwise noted below, hotels charge extra for parking. Rates range from $5 to $15 a night, depending on how close to downtown you are. An 11% room tax and a $1.50 per night occupancy tax will be added to your bill.

Highly recommended lodgings are indicated by a star ★.

Category	Cost*
Very Expensive	over $190
Expensive	$130–$190

Moderate	$100–$130

Inexpensive	under $100

All prices are for a standard double room, excluding 11% room tax.

Capitol Hill

Very Expensive

Hyatt Regency on Capitol Hill. One of the chain's more spartan entries in Washington, this hotel has the typical Hyatt garden atrium but with high-tech edges. Close to Union Station and the Mall, this is a mecca for families and for businesspeople with dealings on the Hill. In 1990 the Hyatt Regency completed a $10 million renovation of all guest rooms. Rooms on the south side have a view of the Capitol dome, which is just a few blocks away. Sunday brunch is popular. *400 New Jersey Ave. NW, 20001, tel. 202/737–1234 or 800/233–1234. 834 rooms, including 31 suites. Facilities: 24-hr room service; 3 restaurants; 2 bars; health club with weight equipment, steam room, sauna, pool; parking. AE, DC, MC, V.*

Expensive

Phoenix Park Hotel. Just steps from Union Station and only four blocks from the Capitol, this high-rise hotel has an Irish club theme and is the home of the Dubliner, one of Washington's best bars. Leather, wood panelling, and leaded glass abound in the bar's re-creation of the decor favored by the 18th-century Irish gentry; but guest rooms are bright, traditionally furnished, and quiet. Penthouse suites have fireplaces. The Powerscourt Restaurant is named after an Irish castle. *520 North Capitol St. NW, 20001, tel. 202/638–6900 or 800/824–5419. 88 rooms, including 6 suites. Facilities: 2 restaurants, complimentary newspaper, valet parking. AE, DC, MC, V.*

Moderate

Quality Hotel Capitol Hill. A good value for the budget-minded traveler, this hotel shares the block with the Hyatt and offers the same views and convenience of location. A complete renovation of the hotel, including all guest rooms, was completed in 1990. *415 New Jersey Ave. NW, 20001, tel. 202/638–1616 or 800/228–5151. 341 rooms, including 5 suites. Facilities: room ser-*

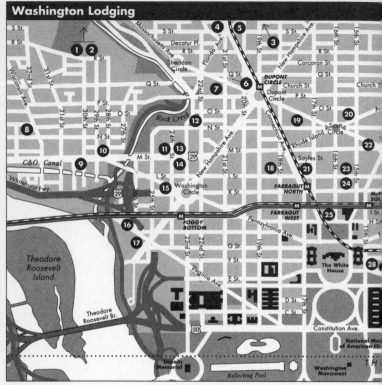

Washington Lodging

ANA Hotel, **11**

Capitol Hilton, **23**

Channel Inn, **35**

Days Inn Connecticut Avenue, **1**

Embassy Row Hotel, **6**

Embassy Suites, **12**

Four Seasons Hotel, **10**

Georgetown Inn, **8**

Georgetown Marbury Hotel, **9**

Grand Hotel, **14**

Grand Hyatt, **26**

Hay-Adams Hotel, **25**

Holiday Inn Crowne Plaza at Metro Center, **27**

Holiday Inn Governor's House, **20**

Hotel Anthony, **18**

Hotel Tabard Inn, **19**

Hotel Washington, **28**

Howard Johnson Kennedy Center, **16**

Hyatt Regency on Capitol Hill, **33**

J.W. Marriott, **30**

Loew's L'Enfant Plaza , **34**

Mayflower Hotel, **21**

Omni Shoreham Hotel, **3**

Park Hyatt Washington, **13**

Phoenix Park Hotel, **31**

Quality Hotel Capitol Hill, **32**

Quality Hotel Central, **4**

The Ritz-Carlton, **6**

Sheraton Carlton Hotel, **24**

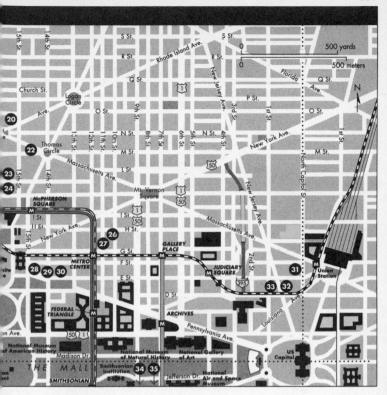

Sheraton
Washington
Hotel, **2**

The Washington
Hilton and
Towers, **5**

Washington
Vista Hotel, **22**

Watergate
Hotel, **17**

The Willard
Inter-
Continental, **29**

Wyndham
Bristol Hotel, **15**

vice *6:30 AM–11 PM, restaurant, outdoor rooftop pool, free parking. AE, DC, MC, V.*

Downtown

Very Expensive **Capitol Hilton.** There are three advantages here: location, location, and location. The busy Capitol Hilton is not only just up the street from official Washington, including the White House and many monuments, it is smack in the middle of the K Street business corridor. Built in 1943 as a Statler Hotel, the building underwent a $55 million renovation that was completed in 1987. Rooms were enlarged by a third. Now the theme is neo–art deco, with torchères, winding staircases, and columns finished with milled cherrywood. Rooms are sleekly furnished in shades of camel, gray, or dusty rose. The new Towers section on the top four floors offers VIP accommodations. Fitness-conscious guests use the state-of-the-art health club. The hotel hosts the annual Gridiron Club dinner, at which the media have roasted every president since Franklin Roosevelt. *1001 16th St. NW, 20036, 202/393–1000 or 800/445–8667. 549 rooms, including 34 suites. Facilities: 24-hr room service; 2 restaurants; valet parking; barber and beauty salon; health club with treadmills, Nautilus equipment, steam room, sauna, tanning bed. AE, DC, MC, V.*

Grand Hyatt. Imagine a 1930s movie-musical set. Studio-built walls of a Mediterranean hillside village rise around a courtyard; a gazebo and curved lounge and dining areas surround a blue lagoon fed by waterfalls. On a small island in the lagoon is a man in black tie playing Cole Porter tunes on a white grand piano. The Hyatt has created just such a fanciful interior in this bustling new high-rise hotel that successfully compensates for the relative drabness of the neighborhood. Opened in June 1987, the Grand is across the street from the Washington Convention Center and just steps away from downtown shopping and theaters. Quiet, contemporary rooms are reached by glass-walled elevators; some suites have Jacuzzis or saunas. Conference suites are popular with businesspeople who may need to meet clients in their rooms. The Zephyr Deli is a popular lunch spot; the Grand Cafe features country breakfasts on weekends. A disco—Impulse—attracts local office workers and conventioners. *1000 H St. NW, 20001, tel. 202/582–1234 or 800/228–9000. 908 rooms, including 61 suites. Facilities: 24-hr room service, 3 restaurants, bar, multilingual staff, health club, valet parking. AE, DC, MC, V.*

★ **Hay-Adams Hotel.** Built in 1927, the Hay-Adams sits upon the site of houses owned by John Hay and Henry Adams, social and political paragons in turn-of-the-century Washington. In its early days the hotel housed Charles Lindbergh and Amelia Earhart; now, corporate executives and lawyers occupy its rooms during the week, and couples and families come on weekends. Italian Renaissance in design, the hotel looks like a mansion in disguise. Seventeenth-century Medici tapestries grace two lobby walls, while the John Hay Room restaurant seems to belong to an English Tudor residence. The guest rooms are the most brightly colored in the city, decorated in 20 different English–country-house schemes. Rooms on the south side have a picture-postcard view of the White House. The hotel's afternoon tea is renowned, and the Adams Room is a popular spot for power breakfasts. The staff is dignified and friendly. *One Lafayette Square, 20006, tel. 202/638–6600 or 800/424–5054. 143 rooms, including 23 suites. Facilities: 24-hr room service, 3 restaurants, bar, valet parking. AE, DC, MC, V.*

J.W. Marriott. Opened in 1984, this large, glossy hotel is in a prime location on Pennsylvania Avenue, close to the White House and next door to the National Theater. The hotel may look impersonal, yet the concierge will gladly make a restaurant reservation for you. The Marriott has served as home-away-from-home for Joan Rivers, the prime minister of Israel, and Egyptian President Hosni Mubarak's delegation; but usually it lodges an equal mix of people traveling for business and pleasure. Rooms are furnished in hotel moderne and quiet colors. The best views are on the Pennsylvania Avenue side. On other sides, you may end up looking across a courtyard at the blank windows of another section of the complex. Guests have indoor access to the National Press Building and the shops and restaurants of National Place. The signature dessert at the Celadon restaurant is Painter's Palette, made of chocolate topped with fruit sorbets. *1331 Pennsylvania Ave. NW, 20004, tel. 202/393–2000 or 800/228–9290. 773 rooms, including 41 suites. Facilities: 24-hr room service, 4 restaurants, bar, health club with Universal weights and stationary bikes, indoor pool, valet parking. AE, DC, MC, V.*

Sheraton Carlton Hotel. Entering the Sheraton Carlton is like stepping into an updated Italian Renaissance mansion: Gilt, carved wood, stone, plaster, and 19th-century details abound. This hotel is in a bustling business sector, yet the rooms are quiet and service is cordial and dignified. Built in 1926, the hotel underwent a $20 million face-lift which began in 1988, in the course of which all rooms were completely refurbished and renovated. The rooms are decorated in pastel colors and are furnished with antiques and reproductions. Each room has a safe. Butler service is available. *923 16th St. NW, 20006, tel. 202/638–2626 or 800/325–3535. 197 rooms, including 13 suites. Facilities: 24-hr room service, personal safes in rooms, 3 telephones and 2 telephone lines in each room, restaurant, bar, exercise room, exercise equipment delivered to room, valet parking. AE, DC, MC, V.*

★ **The Willard Inter-Continental.** "This hotel, in fact, may be much more justly called the center of Washington and the Union than either the Capitol, the White House, or the State Department," Nathaniel Hawthorne wrote while covering the Civil War. Indeed, the Willard, whose present building dates from 1901, welcomed every American president from Franklin Pierce in 1853 to Dwight Eisenhower in the 1950s. Martin Luther King wrote his "I have a dream" speech here. But the huge building fell on hard times and closed in 1968. When renovation began in 1984, grass grew in the rooms and a tree had sprouted in one of the restaurants. The new Willard is a faithful renovation, presenting an opulent, beaux-arts feast to the eye. Even D.C. residents drop in to stroll the famous "Peacock Alley," which runs between the front and back entrances. Rooms are furnished with mahogany Queen Anne reproductions; all have minibar. The sixth floor, which was designed with the help of the Secret Service and the State Department, has lodged 20 heads of state. Two restaurants, the Occidental and the Willard Room, have won nationwide acclaim. *1401 Pennsylvania Ave. NW, 20004, tel. 202/628–9100 or 800/327–0200. 365 rooms, including 37 suites. Eight rooms designed for the handicapped. Facilities: 24-hr room service, 3 restaurants, 2 bars, valet parking. AE, DC, MC, V.*

Expensive **Holiday Inn Crowne Plaza at Metro Center.** "Holiday Inn" has come to be synonymous with standard American motel decor, but this Holiday Inn Crowne Plaza belies all preconceptions, from the enormous mauve marble registration desk to the artwork throughout the hotel especially commissioned from Washington artists. The hotel's restaurant and bar, the Metro Center Grille and Bar, is a handsome two-level facility decorated in mahogany, oak, brass, and marble. The New American cuisine of executive chef Melissa Balinger has made the restaurant a popular downtown lunch and dinner spot for locals as well as guests. The larger-than-average rooms, decorated in mauve and soft blue, are more comfortable than luxurious. Each has a desk and two easy chairs. Two executive floors offer complimentary continental breakfast, courtesy bar, and a private lounge. *775 12th St. NW, 20005, tel. 202/737–2200 or 800/HOLIDAY. 456 rooms, including 12 suites. Facilities: 24-hr room service; valet parking; restaurant; bar; health club with whirlpool, sauna, Lifecycles, StairMaster, rowing machines, Universal weights, aerobics, indoor pool. AE, DC, MC, V.*

Hotel Washington. Since its opening in 1918, this hostelry has been known as the hotel with a view. Washingtonians bring visitors to the outdoor rooftop bar for cocktails and a view of the White House grounds and the Washington Monument. The oldest continuously operating hostelry in the city and now a national landmark, the Hotel Washington sprang from the drawing boards of John Carrere and Thomas Hastings, who designed the New York Public Library. Renovated in 1987, the hotel has retained its Edwardian character; a Gibson girl would not feel out of place in the lobby. The guest rooms, some of which look directly onto the White

House grounds, are furnished with antique reproductions; the windows are festooned with
swags, heavy drapes, and lace underdrapes.
Antique beiges predominate. Suite 506 is where
Elvis Presley stayed on his trips to D.C. *515
15th St. NW, 20004, tel. 202/638–5900. 350
rooms and 17 suites. Facilities: room service 6 AM–midnight, restaurant, outdoor café,
lounge, fitness center. AE, DC, MC, V.*

Mayflower, A Stouffer Hotel. The Mayflower was
opened in 1925 for Calvin Coolidge's inaugural
and continues to be a central part of Washington
life. Guests come from all walks of life; 8% of
them are foreign. The recently renovated, ornate lobby gleams with gilded trim and cherubs
supporting electrified candelabra. About half
the hotel's rooms have been restored with cus-
tom-designed furniture, warmly colored fabrics, full marble bathrooms, and indirect
lighting. The renovation is scheduled to be completed by July of 1992. Seventy-four suites have
the original but nonworking fireplaces. A Japa-
nese-style breakfast is offered, and afternoon
tea is popular. The Mayflower is steps from the
K Street business corridor, the White House,
and Dupont Circle. *1127 Connecticut Ave. NW,
20036, tel. 202/347–3000 or 800/468–3571. 724
rooms, including 83 suites. Facilities: 24-hr
room service, 2 restaurants, bar, shops, access
to National Capital YMCA, parking at nearby
garage. AE, DC, MC, V.*

Washington Vista Hotel. This 14-story member
of the Hilton International family is located in
one of downtown's fastest-developing areas and
is a few blocks from the White House, the Washington Convention Center, and the K Street
business corridor. Designed to look like an urban town square, the Vista features a garden-
courtyard lobby that is flooded by light from a
130-foot window facing M Street. Guest rooms
and restaurants are located in the surrounding
towerlike structures. Opened in 1983, the hotel
has hosted Elizabeth Taylor, Kirk Douglas, and
countless business travelers from the United
States and abroad. Rooms are contemporary in
design and decorated in earth tones, burgundy,
and green. Some face an alley; the hotel doesn't
rent these out unless all other rooms are occupied, and even then guests are warned. The

Presidential Suite and six other suites were designed by Hubert de Givenchy; these have Jacuzzis, French-silk and cotton-blend wall coverings, and original artwork from France. *1400 M St. NW, 20005, tel. 202/429–1700 or 800/ VISTA–DC. 400 rooms, including 14 suites. Facilities: 24-hr room service, 2 restaurants, 2 bars, health club with sauna, multilingual staff, baby-sitting service, valet parking. AE, DC, MC, V.*

Moderate **Holiday Inn Governor's House.** A deluxe Holiday Inn with a sweeping staircase in the lobby, this hotel is close to the White House and Dupont Circle. All guest rooms were refurbished in the spring of 1990. The staff is friendly. *1615 Rhode Island Ave. NW, 20036, tel. 202/296–2100 or 800/821–4367. 152 rooms, including 9 suites; 36 rooms have kitchenettes. Facilities: room service 7 AM–midnight, restaurant, bar, outdoor pool, access to health club, parking. AE, DC, MC, V.*

Hotel Anthony. A good value, this small hotel has a courteous staff, offers the basics in the midst of the K and L streets business district, and is close to the White House. Some rooms have a full kitchen, some a wet bar; king, queen, or extra-long double beds are available. *1823 L St. NW, 20036, tel. 202/223–4320 or 800/424–2970. 99 rooms. Facilities: room service 7 AM–10 PM, 2 restaurants, access to health club, parking. AE, DC, MC, V.*

Dupont Circle

Very Expensive **The Ritz-Carlton.** One of the nicest things to do at the Ritz on a winter day (aside from stay ★ there) is to have a drink or afternoon tea in front of the fire in the warm, woody Fairfax Bar. Exclusive and intimate, the hotel has an English hunt-club theme. European furnishings abound and an extensive collection of 18th- and 19th-century English art, heavy on horses and dogs, graces the walls. This is the home of the pricey Jockey Club restaurant, where crowned heads of Washington like to have lunch (it was one of Nancy Reagan's favorite spots). Lee Iacocca, Carol Burnett, and Eddie Murphy have stayed here. *2100 Massachusetts Ave. NW, 20008, tel. 202/293–2100 or 800/241–3333. 230 rooms, in-*

*cluding 23 suites. Facilities: 24-hr room service,
restaurant, access to health club. AE, DC, MC,
V.*

Expensive **Embassy Row Hotel.** Located near Dupont Circle in a neighborhood of grand houses now mostly used as embassies, museums, and galleries, this hotel is equally convenient for business and vacation trips to Washington. The spacious rooms are decorated in neutral colors and light woods with accents of rich crimson and forest green. The bar is perhaps the coziest in Washington, and the cooking of chef Jim Papovich at Lucie, the hotel's elegant restaurant, has made it a favorite of locals and tourists alike. The roof deck and pool offer a fine view of the city. *2015 Massachusetts Ave. NW, 20036, tel. 202/265–1600 or 800/424–2400. 196 rooms, including 28 suites. Facilities: 24-hr room service, restaurant, bar, rooftop pool, access to health club, valet parking. AE, DC, MC, V.*

★ **The Washington Hilton and Towers.** One of the city's busiest convention hotels, this 24-year-old establishment is as much an event as a place to stay. President George Bush made two appearances here in one week. At any moment, you could run into a leading actor, a cabinet official, six busloads of teenagers from Utah, 500 visiting heart surgeons, or Supreme Court Justice Sandra Day O'Connor, who is among the notables who have played tennis here. Though this Hilton specializes in large groups, individual travelers who like to be where the action is also check in. A $27 million refurbishment was completed in 1988. The light-filled, pastel-colored guest rooms are furnished in hotel moderne and have marble bathrooms. In back of the hotel is a miniresort with a café. Dancing and live music are the draw at Ashby's Club. The hotel is a short walk from the shops and restaurants of Dupont Circle, Embassy Row, the National Zoo, and the Adams-Morgan neighborhood. *1919 Connecticut Ave. NW, 20009, tel. 202/483–3000 or 800/445–8667. 1,150 rooms, including 88 suites. Facilities: 24-hr room service, 3 restaurants (one seasonal), 2 bars, 3 lighted tennis courts, outdoor pool, whirlpool, weight-training equipment, pro shop, flower shop, valet parking. AE, DC, MC, V.*

Inexpensive **Hotel Tabard Inn.** Three Victorian townhouses
★ were linked 70 years ago to form an inn, and the
establishment is still welcoming guests. Named
after the hostelry of Chaucer's *Canterbury Ta-
les*, the hotel is furnished throughout with
broken-in Victorian and American Empire
antiques. A Victorian-inspired carpet cushions
the hallways, which run in intriguing labyrin-
thine patterns. Rooms have phone but no TV.
There is no room service, but the Tabard Inn
Restaurant serves breakfast, lunch, and dinner;
menus feature local ingredients whenever possible. Located on a quiet street, the hotel is a
quick walk to Dupont Circle and the K Street
business district. Reserve at least two weeks in
advance. *1739 N St. NW, 20036, tel. 202/785–
1277. 40 rooms, 23 with private bath. Facilities:
restaurant. MC, V.*

★ **Quality Hotel Central.** A Holiday Inn until 1988,
this high-rise just up the street from Dupont
Circle is one of the city's best values for travelers on a budget. Travelers who can't find rooms
at the Washington Hilton stay here, as well as
families and businesspeople. Rooms are clean,
quiet, and decorated with light colors and blond
wood. Rooms on the western and southern sides
have good views. *1900 Connecticut Ave. NW,
20009, tel. 202/332–9300 or 800/842–4211. 149
rooms. Facilities: room service 7 AM–10 PM, restaurant, outdoor pool, access to health club, free
parking. AE, DC, MC, V.*

Georgetown

Very **Four Seasons Hotel.** A polished staff is at your
Expensive service the moment you approach the doors of
★ this contemporary hotel conveniently situated
between Georgetown and Foggy Bottom. The
Four Seasons is a gathering place for Washington's elite. Rooms, all of which have a minibar,
are traditionally furnished in light colors. The
quieter rooms face the courtyard; others have a
view of the C & O Canal. The restaurant, Aux
Beaux Champs, is highly esteemed by locals.
Afternoon tea is served in the Garden Terrace
Lounge. The Four Seasons is also home to the
private nightclub Desiree, which is open to hotel guests, and to what is perhaps the poshest
health club of any hotel in America. Guests may

choose between watching movies on a VCR or listening to French lessons on a Walkman as they burn calories on their exercise bikes. *2800 Pennsylvania Ave., NW, 20007, tel. 202/342–0444 or 800/332–3442. 197 rooms, including 30 suites. Facilities: 24-hr room service, 2 restaurants, bar, nightclub, health club with pool, multilingual staff, valet parking. AE, DC, MC, V.*

Expensive   **Georgetown Inn.** With an atmosphere like a gentlemen's sporting club of 80 years ago, the inn recreates the intimacy and quiet of a small European hotel. The architecture is redbrick and 18th-century in flavor, appropriate to its setting. This is the home of the Georgetown Bar & Grill, whose bar is particularly renowned for lavish appetizers. Traditionally furnished rooms, in apple-green or pink color schemes, are un-hotellike. *1310 Wisconsin Ave. NW, 20007, tel. 202/333–8900 or 800/424–2979. 95 rooms, including 10 suites. Facilities: room service 7 AM–11 PM, restaurant, bar, access to exercise classes, valet parking. AE, DC, MC, V.*

Georgetown Marbury Hotel. A small, colonial-style hotel in the midst of the city's liveliest neighborhoods, the redbrick Marbury is undergoing extensive renovation. Those who value total quiet may want to request one of the 40 rooms underground; the only windows in these rooms face a hallway that has the appearance of a narrow lane. Other rooms have views of the C&O Canal or busy M Street. A colonial theme predominates; rooms have low ceilings and country cotton prints. The Paradox Brasserie and Tavern is decorated in a tropical theme. Opened in 1981, the hotel is popular with Europeans, sports figures, and devotees of Georgetown. *3000 M St. NW, 20007, tel. 202/726–5000 or 800/368–5922. 164 rooms, including 9 suites. Facilities: room service 7 AM–10:30 PM, 2 restaurants, 2 bars, outdoor pool, access to health club, valet parking. AE, DC, MC, V.*

Southwest

Expensive   **Loew's L'Enfant Plaza.** After a day of tramping through the museums on the nearby Smithsonian Mall, families return here to collapse and, during the warmer months, take a dip in the inviting rooftop pool. Loew's is an oasis of velvet and chintz in L'Enfant Plaza, a concrete collection of office buildings with underground shops that is D.C.'s version of Brasilia. Travelers with government business stay here, too, in close proximity to several agency headquarters and just down the street from Capitol Hill. Each room has a fully stocked liquor cabinet and a refrigerator. A $17 million refurbishing and remodeling was completed in 1990. Service is friendly, and Cafe Pierre serves an international menu at lunch and dinner. *480 L'Enfant Plaza SW, 20024, tel. 202/484–1000 or 800/223–0888. 372 rooms, including 22 suites. Facilities: 24-hr room service, VCRs, 3 phones with 2 lines, TV and radio in bathrooms, 3 restaurants, 2 bars, year-round rooftop pool, health club, parking. AE, DC, MC, V.*

Inexpensive **Channel Inn.** This informal establishment on an inlet of the Potomac offers views of bobbing boats and tranquil parkland across the water. Within walking distance of Arena Stage and a 15-minute walk away from the Mall, the Channel Inn still seems far-removed from official Washington. The L'Enfant Plaza subway stop is about a 15-minute walk away; buses are also nearby. Air traffic can be noisy during the daytime. All rooms have a balcony or deck area and separate vanity area; 37 have a river view. A complete renovation, including all rooms and baths, was completed in 1990. *650 Water St. SW, 20024, tel. 202/554–2400 or 800/368–5668. 100 rooms, including 2 suites. Facilities: room service 6:30 AM–11 PM, restaurant, bar, coffee shop, outdoor pool, free parking. AE, DC, MC, V.*

Upper Connecticut Avenue

Very Expensive **Sheraton Washington Hotel.** A veritable city on a hill, this is Washington's largest hotel. It consists of an "old town"—a 1920s redbrick structure that used to be an apartment building—and the modern sprawl of the new, convention-ready, main complex. The 250 rooms and the public areas of the 10-story old section were renovated in 1988; they are furnished traditionally in soft colors and have large closets. Rooms in the nine-year-old new section are contemporary, with chrome and glass touches. Most rooms have a good view. The courtyard is graced by a modernistic fountain; the hotel also has an airy atrium and plush, sunken seating-areas galore. Pastry chef Wolfgang Friedrich has a carry-out shop on the premises: Calorie-watchers beware. The hotel is close to the National Zoo and just a few yards from the Woodley Park Metrorail station. *2660 Woodley Rd. NW, 20008, tel. 202/328-2000 or 800/325-3535. 1,505 rooms, including 124 suites. Facilities: 24-hr room service, 4 restaurants, 2 bars, nightclub, health club with Universal weights and stationary bikes, 2 outdoor pools, baby-sitting service, parking. AE, DC, MC, V.*

Expensive **Omni Shoreham Hotel.** You're in good company
★ when you check in at this grand, 1930s Art Deco–Renaissance hotel. The Beatles stayed here on their first U.S. tour. John Kennedy courted Jackie in the Blue Room cabaret, where Judy Garland, Marlene Dietrich, and Maurice Chevalier once appeared. Resembling an old-time resort, this hotel overlooks Rock Creek Park and its jogging and bike paths. In back is the pool, where you can look out to a sweeping lawn and woods beyond. Adding to the '30s tropical-resort atmosphere are mock bamboo furnishings in the entrance area and doormen wearing pith helmets during the warmer months. The rooms are large and light-filled. Some have fireplaces; half overlook the park. Comedienne Joan Cushing holds forth in the Marquee Cabaret (the Blue Room is now a meeting room). The loyal staff takes your stay personally. Situated in a fairly quiet area, the Omni is close to the Adams-Morgan neighborhood, Dupont Circle, and the National Zoo. *2500 Calvert St. NW, 20008, tel. 202/234-0700 or 800/834-6664. 770 rooms, including 50 suites. Facilities: room service 6 AM–11 PM, 2 restaurants, bar, snack counter, cabaret, outdoor pool, 3 lighted tennis courts, shuffleboard court, horseshoe pits, half-size basketball court, fitness center, shops, art gallery, parking. AE, DC, MC, V.*

Inexpensive **Days Inn Connecticut Avenue.** An alternative for those who prefer to stay away from the downtown hustle and bustle, this Day's Inn is on a wide avenue in a largely residential area. A subway line close by provides quick transportation to the National Zoo (two stops away) and all of Washington's major attractions. The University of the District of Columbia is next door. Rooms have standard hotel furnishings and may be small. A complimentary Continental breakfast is provided in the lower lobby. There are several cafés nearby. *4400 Connecticut Ave. NW, 20008, tel. 202/244–5600. 155 rooms, including 5 suites. Facilities: free parking. Room service from nearby Espresso Café is available. AE, DC, MC, V.*

West End/Foggy Bottom

Very Expensive ★

ANA Hotel. A Westin hotel before it was purchased by the Japanese ANA company in 1990, this establishment is a stylish combination of the contemporary and the traditional. Set around a courtyard, the ANA is filled with modern interpretations of Gallic elegance, with a soupçon of Italian classicism. The opening scenes of the movie *Broadcast News* were filmed in the auditorium. Built in 1985, the ANA offers bright, airy, traditionally furnished rooms decorated in greens, blues, and burnished oranges. Each room is supplied with terry-cloth bathrobes and a minibar. About a third of the rooms have a view of the central courtyard. The hotel's informal restaurant, the Bistro, has the flavor of 19th-century Paris and contains an antique mahogany bar. The state-of-the-art health club includes rowing machines, a cross-country ski simulator, treadmills, Nautilus equipment, a lap pool, and a café. The hotel is steps from Georgetown, Rock Creek Park, and the Kennedy Center. *2401 M St. NW, 20037, tel. 202/429–2400 or 800/228–3000. 416 rooms, including 10 suites. Facilities: 24-hr room service, 2 restaurants, bar, café, beauty salon, valet parking. AE, DC, MC, V.*

Grand Hotel. Probably the least known of Washington's luxury hotels, this hotel occupies its prime corner in the West End with an old-world assurance that has made it a favorite of international visitors. Its rooms, although not enormous, are impressive for their comfort and their anticipation of guests' needs. Decorated in light colors that give an impression of airiness and space, each room has an executive-size desk equipped with a two-line telephone. Each bathroom has floor-to-ceiling marble walls, a sunken tub, separate shower, television speaker, and extension telephone. Eight of the hotel's suites have working wood-burning fireplaces. The staff is extraordinarily well trained, and the emphasis on efficient, friendly, and discrete service is apparent in every department. *2350 M St. NW, 20037, tel. 202/429–0100 or 800/848–0016. 263 rooms, including 26 suites. Facilities: 24-hr room service, 3 restaurants, bar, exercise room, outdoor heated pool, valet parking, laundry and dry-cleaning service. AE, DC, MC, V.*

Park Hyatt. A notable collection of modern art adorns this West End hotel, built in 1986. The interior of its main level is built of stone and polished marble, and guests walk on carpeting so thick it almost bounces. Bronzes, chinoiserie, and a fortune teller at tea in the main-floor lounge are a few of the Old-World touches that offset the spareness of the hotel's design. The rooms are a blend of traditional and contemporary elements and contain reproductions of Chinese antiques from Washington museum collections. Fruit and cookies are provided in each room. A special touch, unique in the city, are the upholstered benches along the rear wall of the elevators. The staff has a "never say no" policy, and cars left overnight are washed. *1201 24th St. NW, 20037, tel. 202/789–1234 or 800/ 228–9000. 224 rooms, including 132 bedroom suites. Facilities: 24-hr room service; restaurant; outdoor café (in season); bar; health club with indoor pool, Jacuzzi, and Nautilus equipment; beauty salon, valet parking. AE, DC, MC, V.*

★ **Watergate Hotel.** The internationally famous Watergate, its distinctive sawtooth design a landmark along the Potomac, completed a $14 million renovation in 1988 and is now offering guests a taste of old-English gentility. Scenic murals and a portrait of Queen Elizabeth contribute to the effect. The rooms here are among the largest in Washington. All have live plants or fresh flowers, many have balconies, and most have striking river views. The Jean-Louis restaurant has the only two-star Michelin chef in the United States. The hotel is accustomed to serving the world's elite, but it also welcomes vacationing families and couples on getaway weekends. Part of the exclusive Watergate apartment-and-commercial complex, the hotel is next door to the Kennedy Center and a short walk from Georgetown. *2650 Virginia Ave. NW, 20037, tel. 202/965–2300 or 800/424–2736. 237 rooms, including 160 suites. Facilities: 24-hr room service; 2 restaurants; 2 bars; health club with weights, stationary bikes, steam room, sauna, and indoor pool; complimentary limousine service to Capitol Hill or downtown Mon.–Fri.; valet parking. AE, DC, MC, V.*

Expensive **Embassy Suites.** The hodgepodge of decorative details and cinderblock construction suggest the hanging gardens of Babylon reconstructed in a suburban shopping mall. In the atrium, waterfalls gush, tall palms loom, and plants drip over balconies. Classical columns are mixed with plaster lions and huge Asian temple lights. Ducks swim in the lagoon, and a white rabbit capers nearby, to the delight of children and many grown-ups. Businesspeople flock to the hotel during the week, but it is also ideal for families. Each suite, furnished in neo–art deco, has two remote-control TVs, as well as a wet bar, microwave, coffee-maker, and queen-size sofabed. Complimentary cocktails and cooked-to-order breakfast are served in the atrium. The Italian restaurant, Panevino, has received favorable reviews. Situated in a fairly quiet enclave in the West End, Embassy Suites is within walking distance of Georgetown, the Kennedy Center, and Dupont Circle. *1250 22nd St. NW, 20037, tel. 202/857–3388, 800/EMBASSY, or 800/458–5848 in Canada. 318 suites. Facilities: room service 11–11; restaurant; health club with weight-lifting equipment, treadmills, indoor pool, and sauna; parking. AE, DC, MC, V.*

Wyndham Bristol Hotel. This hotel doesn't offer much in the way of views, but the location is excellent: Located midway between the White House and Georgetown, the Wyndham is a favorite place for movie and theater people because the Kennedy Center is just a few blocks away. The rooms here are quiet, although the building is bordered on two sides by major thoroughfares. The hotel looks as if it belongs to someone who collects Chinese porcelain: A whole cabinet-full greets guests on arrival in the small, quiet lobby. The rest of the hotel, created in 1984 from an apartment building, is English in decor; each room has a butler's table. *2430 Pennsylvania Ave. NW, 20037, tel. 202/ 955–6400, 800/822–4200, or in Canada 800/631– 4200. 240 rooms, including 22 suites. Facilities: room service 7:30 AM–10:30 PM, 2 restaurants (with seasonal outdoor café), bar, access to health club, valet parking, garage. AE, DC, MC, V.*

Inexpensive **Howard Johnson Kennedy Center.** This 10-story lodge offers HoJo reliability in a location close to the Kennedy Center, the Watergate complex, and Georgetown. Rooms are large and comfortable, and each has a refrigerator. *2601 Virginia Ave. NW, 20037, tel. 202/965–2700 or 800/654– 2000. 192 rooms. Facilities: room service 6 AM– 11 PM, restaurant, rooftop pool, free parking for cars only (no vans). AE, DC, MC, V.*

6 The Arts and Nightlife

The Arts

by John F. Kelly

Friday's *Washington Post* "Weekend" section is the best guide to events for the weekend and the coming week. The *Post*'s daily "Guide to the Lively Arts" also outlines cultural events in the city. The *Washington Times* "Weekend" section comes out on Thursday. The free weekly *City Paper* hits the streets on Thursday and covers the entertainment scene well. You might also consult the "City Lights" section in the monthly *Washingtonian* magazine.

Any search for cultured entertainment should start at the **John F. Kennedy Center for the Performing Arts** (New Hampshire Ave. and Rock Creek Parkway NW). The Kennedy Center is actually four stages under one roof: the **Concert Hall,** home park of the National Symphony Orchestra; the 2,200-seat **Opera House,** the setting for ballet, modern dance, grand opera, and large-scale musicals; the **Eisenhower Theater,** usually used for drama; and the **Terrace Theater,** an intimate space designed by Philip Johnson that showcases experimental works and chamber groups. For information call 202/467–4600 or 800/444–1324.

Tickets Tickets to most events are available by calling or visiting each venue's box office.

Metro Center TicketPlace sells half-price, day-of-performance tickets for selected shows; a "menu board" lists available performances. Only cash is accepted for same-day tickets; cash and credit cards may be used for full-price, advance tickets. *12th and F streets NW, tel. 202/ TICKETS. Open Tues–Fri. noon–4, Sat. 11–5. Tickets for Sunday performances sold on Saturday.*

TicketCenter (202/432–0200 or 800/448–9009) takes phone charges for events around the city.

Theater

Commercial Theaters and Companies **Arena Stage** (6th St. and Maine Ave. SW, tel. 202/488–3300) presents a wide-ranging season in its three theaters: the theater-in-the-round Arena, the proscenium Kreeger, and the cabaret-style Old Vat Room.

Ford's Theatre (511 10th St. NW, tel. 202/347–4833) is host mainly to musicals, many with family appeal.

National Theatre (1321 E St. NW, tel. 202/628–6161) presents pre- and post-Broadway shows.

Shakespeare Theatre at the Folger (201 East Capitol St. SE, tel. 202/546–4000) presents works in a replica of an Elizabethan inn-yard theater, reminiscent of Shakespeare's Globe.

Small Theaters and Companies

Source Theatre (1835 14th St. NW, tel. 202/462–1073) presents established plays with a sharp satirical edge and modern interpretations of classics.

Studio Theatre (1333 P St. NW, tel. 202/332–3300) mounts an eclectic season of classic and off-beat plays.

Washington Stage Guild (924 G St. NW, tel. 202/529–2084) tackles the classics—from George Bernard Shaw to Samuel Beckett—as well as more contemporary fare.

Woolly Mammoth's (1401 Church St. NW, tel. 202/393–3939) unusual, imaginatively produced shows have earned good reviews.

Music

Orchestra

The National Symphony Orchestra's (tel. 202/416–8100) season at the Kennedy Center extends from September to June. During the summer, the NSO performs at Wolf Trap and presents concerts on the West Terrace of the Capitol on Memorial Day and Labor Day weekends and on July 4th. One of the cheapest ways to hear—if not necessarily see—Mstislav Rostropovich and the NSO perform in the Kennedy Center Concert Hall is to get a $6 "obstructed view" ticket.

Concert Halls

Capital Centre (1 Harry Truman Dr., Landover, MD, tel. 301/350–3400 or 202/432–0200) is the area's top venue for big-name pop, rock, and rap acts.

D.A.R. Constitution Hall (18th and D Sts. NW, tel. 202/638–2661) hosts visiting performers, from jazz to pop to rap.

Merriweather Post Pavilion (tel. 301/982–1800 or 301/596–0660 off season), an hour north of Washington, in Columbia, Maryland, is an outdoor pavilion with some covered seating.

The National Gallery of Art (6th St. and Constitution Ave. NW, tel. 202/737–4215) hosts free classical music concerts in the venerable West Building's West Garden Court on Sunday evening from October to June.

The Smithsonian Institution (tel. 202/357–2700) presents an amazing assortment of music—both free and ticketed. The Smithsonian's Resident Associate Program (tel. 202/357–3030) offers everything from a cappella groups to Cajun zydeco bands, many of which perform in the National Museum of Natural History's Baird Auditorium.

Wolf Trap Farm Park (1551 Trap Rd., Vienna, VA, tel. 703/255–1860) is a national park dedicated to the performing arts. On its grounds is the **Filene Center** (tel. 703/255–1868), an outdoor theater that is the scene of pop, jazz, opera, ballet, and dance performances each June through September. The rest of the year, the intimate, indoor **Barns at Wolf Trap** (tel. 703/938–2404) hosts folk and acoustic acts.

Chamber Music **Corcoran Gallery of Art** (17th St. and New York Ave. NW, tel. 202/638–3211). Hungary's Takacs String Quartet and the Cleveland Quartet, playing on matched sets of Amati and Stradivarius string instruments owned by the gallery, are among the groups that appear in the Corcoran's Musical Evening Series. Concerts are followed by a reception with the artists.

Folger Shakespeare Library (201 East Capitol St. SE, tel. 202/544–7077). Now in its 15th season, the Folger Shakespeare Library's internationally acclaimed resident chamber-music ensemble regularly presents a selection of instrumental and vocal pieces from the medieval, Renaissance, and baroque periods, during a season that runs from October to May.

National Academy of Sciences (2101 Constitution Ave. NW, tel. 202/334–2000). Free performances by such groups as the Juilliard String Quartet and the Beaux Arts Trio are given October through May in the academy's acoustically nearly perfect auditorium. In 1992 the academy will also host programs normally held in the Library of Congress Jefferson Building, while that space undergoes renovation.

Phillips Collection (1600–1612 21st St. NW, tel.

202/387–2151). The long, panelled music room of gallery founder Duncan Phillip's home is the setting for Sunday afternoon recitals from September through May. Chamber groups from around the world perform; May is devoted to performing artists from the Washington area. Arrive early for the 5 PM concerts.

Performance Series
Armed Forces Concert Series. From June to August, service bands from all four branches of the military perform nightly, Sunday through Friday evenings, on the West Terrace of the Capitol and at the Sylvan Theater on the Washington Monument grounds. The traditional band concerts include marches, patriotic numbers, and some classical music. The bands often perform at other locations throughout the year. *For information: Air Force, tel. 202/767–5658; Army, tel. 703/696–3399; Navy, tel. 202/433–2525; Marines, tel. 202/433–4011.*

Carter Barron Amphitheater (16th St. and Colorado Ave. NW, tel. 202/829–3200 or 202/619–7222). On Saturday and Sunday nights from mid-June to August this lovely, 4,250-seat outdoor theater in Rock Creek Park plays host to pop, jazz, gospel, and rhythm and blues artists such as Chick Corea, Nancy Wilson, and Tito Puente.

Sylvan Theater (Washington Monument grounds, tel. 202/619–7225 or 202/619–7222). On Wednesday there's dancing to big-band and swing music, and from June to August, service bands play Thursday, Friday, and Sunday–Tuesday.

Opera

Summer Opera Theater Company (Hartke Theater, Catholic University, tel. 202/526–1669). This independent professional company mounts two fully staged productions each July and August.

Washington Opera (tel. 202/416–7800 or 800/87–OPERA). Seven operas—presented in their original languages with English supertitles—are performed each season (November to March) in the Kennedy Center's Opera House and Eisenhower Theater.

Dance

Dance Place (3225 8th St. NE, tel. 202/269–1600). This studio theater, which presented its first performance in 1980, annually hosts a wide assortment of modern and ethnic dance.

The Washington Ballet (tel. 202/362–3606). In October, February, and May this contemporary ballet company dances selections from the works of such choreographers as George Balanchine and Paul Taylor, mainly at the Kennedy Center. Each December, the Washington Ballet presents *The Nutcracker*.

Film

Washington has a wealth of first-run movie theaters, in the city and in nearby suburbs:

Several Washington theaters screen revivals and foreign, independent, and avant-garde films.

More than 700 different movies—including contemporary and classic foreign and American films—are shown each year at the **American Film Institute's** (Kennedy Center, tel. 202/785–4600 or 4601) theater in the Kennedy Center. Filmmakers and actors are often present to discuss their work.

Washington's home for alternative cinema, the **Biograph** (2819 M St. NW, recorded information tel. 202/333–2696) presents a mixture of first-run and repertory domestic and foreign films that have in common "their position out of the mainstream."

The Key (1222 Wisconsin Ave. NW, tel. 202/333–5100) specializes in foreign films and presents an annual animation festival.

Nightlife

Many Washington night spots are clustered in a few key areas, simplifying things for the visitor who enjoys bar-hopping. Georgetown, in northwest Washington, leads the pack with an explosion of bars, nightclubs, and restaurants on M Street east and west of Wisconsin Avenue and on Wisconsin Avenue north of M Street. A half dozen Capitol Hill bars can be found on a stretch of Pennsylvania Avenue between 2nd and 4th streets SE. There is another high-density nightlife area around the intersection of 19th and M streets NW.

As for music, Washington audiences are catholic in their tastes and so are Washington's music promoters. That means you can hear funk at a rock club, blues at a jazz club, and calypso at a reggae club. Your best bet is to consult Friday's "Weekend" section in the *Washington Post* and the free, weekly *City Paper*. It's also a good idea to call clubs ahead of time to find out who's on that night and what sort of music will be played.

Bars and Lounges

Brickskeller. A beer lover's mecca, this is the place to go when you want something more exotic than a Bud Lite. More than 500 brands of beer are for sale—from Central American lagers to U.S. microbrewed ales. Bartenders oblige beercan collectors by opening the containers from the bottom. *1523 22nd St. NW, tel. 202/293–1885. Open Mon.–Thurs. 11:30 AM–2 AM, Fri. 11:30 AM–3 AM, Sat. 6 PM–3 AM, Sun. 6 PM–2 AM. AE, DC, MC, V.*

Champions. Walls covered with jerseys, pucks, bats, and balls, and the evening's big game on the big-screen TV, leave little doubt that this popular Georgetown establishment is a sportslover's bar. Ballpark-style food enhances the mood. *1206 Wisconsin Ave. NW, tel. 202/965–4005. Open Mon.–Thurs. 5 PM–2 AM, Fri. 5 PM–3 AM, Sat. 11:30 AM–3 AM, Sun. 11:30 AM–2 AM. One-drink minimum Fri. and Sat. after 10 PM. AE, MC, V.*

The Dubliner. Snug, panelled rooms; thick, tasty Guinness; and nightly live entertainment are the main attractions at Washington's premier Irish pub. You don't have to be Irish to enjoy it, as scores of staffers from nearby Capitol Hill attest. *520 North Capitol St. NW, tel. 202/737–3773. Open Mon.–Thurs. 11 AM–2 AM, Fri. 11 AM–3 AM, Sat. 7:30 AM–3 AM, Sun. 7:30 AM–2 AM. AE, DC, MC, V.*

F. Scott's. Elegant art deco surroundings and dancing to music from the '30s and '40s make this upper-Georgetown night spot popular with

older, well-dressed Gatsbys and Daisys. *1232
36th St. NW, tel. 202/342–0009. Open Tues.–
Sat. 7 PM–2 AM, Fri. and Sat. 7 PM–3 AM. AE,
DC, MC, V.*

Hawk 'n' Dove. A friendly neighborhood bar in a
neighborhood coincidentally dominated by the
Capitol building. Regulars include political
types, lobbyists, and well-behaved Marines
(from a nearby barracks). *329 Pennsylvania
Ave. SE, tel. 202/543–3300. Open Sun.–Thurs.
10 AM–2 AM, Fri. and Sat. 10 AM–3 AM. AE, DC,
MC, V.*

Sign of the Whale. The best hamburger in town
is available at the bar in this well-known post-
Preppie/neo-Yuppie haven. *1825 M St. NW, tel.
202/223–4152. Open daily 11:30 AM–2 AM. DC,
MC, V.*

Cabarets

Chelsea's. The musical political satire of the
Capitol Steps, a group of current and former
Hill staffers, is presented on Fridays and Saturdays. (The troupe's name comes from a pur-
ported trysting spot of politician John Jenrette
and wife Rita.) *1055 Thomas Jefferson St. NW,
tel. 202/298–8222 or 703/683–8330. Shows Fri.
and Sat. at 7:30. Ticket charge. Reservations required. AE, MC, V.*

Gross National Product. The titles of a few past
shows should give you an idea of what this irrev-
erent comedy troupe is up to: "BushCapades:
An Administration on Thin Ice," "Man Without
a Contra," and "The Phantom of the White
House." GNP, which the *Washington Post* has
compared to the original cast of "Saturday
Night Live," performs at the Bayou in Georgetown. *3135 K St. NW, tel. 202/783–7212. Show
Sat. 7:30. Ticket charge. Reservations suggested. MC, V.*

Marquee Cabaret. Funnylady Joan Cushing as-
sumes the character of quintessential Washington insider "Mrs. Foggy-bottom" and, with a
small cast, pokes fun at well-known political figures in satirical skit and song. *Omni-Shoreham
Hotel, 2500 Calvert St. NW, tel. 202/745–1023.
Shows Thurs.–Sat. 9 PM. Ticket charge. Reservations required. AE, DC, MC, V.*

Comedy Clubs

Comedy Cafe. Local and national comics appear at this club in the heart of downtown. Thursday is open-mike night; on Friday and Saturday, the pros take the stage. *1520 K St. NW, tel. 202/638-JOKE. Shows Thurs. 8:30; Fri. 8:30 and 10:30; Sat. 7, 9, and 11. Some shows Sun. Cover charge. AE, DC, MC, V.*

Garvin's Comedy Clubs. Garvin's has become the McDonald's of laughs in the Washington area, serving jokes at various locations. In addition to its downtown club, the comedy powerhouse rotates comics through restaurants and hotels in the Washington area and up and down the mid-Atlantic. *1335 Greens Ct. NW (L St. between 13th and 14th Sts. NW), tel. 202/783-2442. Shows Tues.–Thurs. 8:30; Fri. 8:30 and 10:30; Sat. 7:30, 9:30, and 11:30. Cover charge. Reservations required. AE, MC, V. Also: Shows Fri. and Sat. at Phillips Flagship Restaurant, 900 Water St. NW; and Alexandria Ramada Inn, I–395 and Seminary Rd., Alexandria, VA.*

Acoustic/Folk/Country

Afterwords. This place could just as easily be called Before words or During words, shoehorned as it is in a bookshop near Dupont Circle. Folkish acts entertain browsing bohemian bookworms as well as patrons seated at a cozy in-store cafe. *1517 Connecticut Ave. NW, tel. 202/387-1462. Open Tues.–Thurs. 7:30 AM–1 AM and from Fri. 7:30 AM to Mon. 1 AM. AE, MC, V.*

Birchmere. The best place in the area to hear acoustic folk and bluegrass acts is in an unpretentious suburban strip shopping center. Favorite sons the Seldom Scene are Thursday-night regulars. Audiences come to listen, and the management politely insists on no distracting chatter. *3901 Mt. Vernon Ave., Alexandria, VA, tel. 703/549-5919. Open Tues.–Sat. 7 PM–11:30 PM. MC, V.*

Zed Restaurant. Can cowboy hats and boots exist in the same city as Brooks Brothers suits? A visit to Zed proves that they can. Each evening, bands in this suburban Virginia night spot play hits from Nashville and other points south and

west. Two-stepping is encouraged. *6151 Rich-
mond Hwy., Alexandria, VA, tel. 703/768–5558.
Open daily 11 AM–2 AM. Dress: casual but neat.
AE, MC, V.*

Dance Clubs

Hoofers who prefer "touch" dancing should call
the recorded information line of the very active
Washington Area Swing Dance Committee (tel.
301/779–0234). The group organizes monthly
boogie woogie, jitterbug, and swing workshops
and dances.

Fifth Column. A trendy, well-dressed crowd
waits in line to dance to the latest releases from
London and Europe on three floors of this converted bank. Avant-garde art installations
change every four months. *915 F St. NW, tel.
202/393–3632. Open Sun.–Thurs. 10 PM–2 AM,
Fri.–Sat. 10 PM–3 AM. Cover charge. AE, MC,
V.*

Kilimanjaro. Deep in ethnically diverse Adams-
Morgan, the Kilimanjaro specializes in "international" music from the Caribbean and Africa.
Every Thursday there's a local reggae band,
and international artists often perform on Sunday. *1724 California St. NW, tel. 202/328–3838.
Open Mon.–Thurs. 5 PM–2 AM, Fri. 5 PM–4:30
AM, Sat. 6 PM–4 AM, Sun. 6 PM–2 AM. Cover
charge. MC, V.*

Tracks. A gay club with a large contingent of
straight regulars, this warehouse-district disco
has one of the largest dance floors in town and
stays open late. *1111 1st St. SE, tel. 202/488–
3320. Open Tues. 6 PM–2 AM, Wed. and Thurs. 6
PM–4 AM, Fri. and Sat. 6 PM–6 AM, Sun. noon–4
AM. Cover charge Wed.–Sun. after 9 PM. No
credit cards.*

Jazz Clubs

Blues Alley. The restaurant turns out Creole
cooking, while cooking on stage are such nation-
ally known performers as Charlie Byrd and
Ramsey Lewis. You can come for just the show,
but those who come for a meal get better seats.
*Rear 1073 Wisconsin Ave. NW, tel. 202/337–
4141. Open Mon.–Thurs. 6 PM–midnight, Fri.
and Sat. 6 PM–2 AM. Shows at 8 and 10, plus*

midnight shows Fri. and Sat. Cover charge and $5 food/drink minimum. AE, DC, MC, V.

One Step Down. Low-ceilinged, intimate, and boasting the best jazz jukebox in town, this small club books talented local artists, the occasional national act, and is the venue of choice for many New York jazz masters. It's frayed and smoky, the way a jazz club should be. *2517 Pennsylvania Ave. NW, tel. 202/331–8863. Open Mon.–Thurs. 10 PM–2 AM, Fri. and Sat. 10 PM–3 AM, Sun. noon–2 AM. Cover charge and minimum. AE, DC, MC, V.*

Rock, Pop, and Rhythm and Blues Clubs

The Bayou. Located in Georgetown, underneath the Whitehurst Freeway, the Bayou is a Washington fixture that showcases national acts on weeknights and local talent on weekends. Bands cover rock in all its permutations: pop rock, hard rock, soft rock, new rock, and classic rock. Tickets are available at the door or through TicketCenter. *3135 K St. NW, tel. 202/333–2897. Open daily 8 PM–2 AM. Cover charge. No credit cards.*

Club Soda. The room and dance floor are tiny, but this is one of the best places in town to hear cover bands perform consistently accurate oldies music (Wednesday through Sunday). A DJ spins the real thing next door. *3433 Connecticut Ave. NW, tel. 202/244–3189. Open Mon.–Thurs. 4 PM–2 AM, Fri. 4 PM–3 AM, Sat. 7 PM–3 AM, Sun. 7 PM–2 AM. Cover charge on weekends. No credit cards.*

d.c. space. Early in the evening this downtown artists' bar features cabaret shows. After that, bands take the small stage and treat the casually dressed audience to punk, new wave, and various other interesting musical forms. *433 7th St. NW, tel. 202/347–4960. Open Mon.–Thurs. 11:30 AM–2 AM, Fri. 11:30 AM–3 AM, Sat. 6 PM–3 AM. Cover charge. AE, MC, V.*

9:30 Club. This trendy club in the center of Washington's old downtown books an eclectic mix of local, national, and international artists, most of whom play what used to be known as "new wave" music (from the Fleshtones, Guadalcanal Diary, and Robyn Hitchcock, among others). The regulars dress to be seen, but visitors won't feel out of place. Get tickets at the door or through Ticketron. *930 F St. NW, tel. 202/393-0930. Hours vary according to shows but generally open Tues. 8 PM–2 AM, Wed.–Thurs. 4 PM–2 AM, Fri. 4 PM–3 AM, Sat. 9 PM–3 AM. Cover charge. No credit cards.*

Index

Personal Itinerary

Departure *Date*

Time

Transportation

Arrival *Date*   *Time*

Departure *Date*   *Time*

Transportation

Arrival *Date*   *Time*

Departure *Date*   *Time*

Transportation

Arrival *Date*   *Time*

Departure *Date*   *Time*

Transportation

Personal Itinerary

Arrival	*Date*	*Time*
Departure	*Date*	*Time*
Transportation		

Arrival	*Date*	*Time*
Departure	*Date*	*Time*
Transportation		

Arrival	*Date*	*Time*
Departure	*Date*	*Time*
Transportation		

Arrival	*Date*	*Time*
Departure	*Date*	*Time*
Transportation		

Personal Itinerary

Arrival *Date*   *Time*

Departure *Date*   *Time*

Transportation

Arrival *Date*   *Time*

Departure *Date*   *Time*

Transportation

Arrival *Date*   *Time*

Departure *Date*   *Time*

Transportation

Arrival *Date*   *Time*

Departure *Date*   *Time*

Transportation

Adresses	*Adresses*
Name	*Name*
Address	*Address*
Telephone	*Telephone*
Name	*Name*
Address	*Address*
Telephone	*Telephone*
Name	*Name*
Address	*Address*
Telephone	*Telephone*
Name	*Name*
Address	*Address*
Telephone	*Telephone*
Name	*Name*
Address	*Address*
Telephone	*Telephone*
Name	*Name*
Address	*Address*
Telephone	*Telephone*